The Book of Language

THE BOOK OF LANGUAGE

Exploring the Spiritual Vocabulary of Islām

Kabir Helminski

With an essay on *Truth and Knowledge*
by Prince Ghazi Bin Muḥammad
and Appendices
by Jeremy Henzell-Thomas

THE BOOK FOUNDATION
WATSONVILLE, CALIFORNIA
BRISTOL, ENGLAND

THE BOOK FOUNDATION
www.thebook.org

Publication Design & Cover Art by Threshold Productions and Ahmed Moustafa.

First Book Foundation edition published 2006.

British Library Cataloguing in Publication Data
A catalogue record of this book is available from the British Library

Library of Congress Cataloging-in-Publication Data

Watsonville, California; Bristol, England: The Book Foundation, 2006.

ISBN 1-904510-16-7 9781904510161
1. Islamic Doctrines. 2. Islamic terminology
I. Kabir Helminski II. The Book Foundation

Acknowledgments

The editor wishes to thank Talal and Nadia Zahid for their foresight and generosity, Jeremy Henzell-Thomas for his continual discussion in the field of language; Robert Crane for his many insights into Islamic tradition; James Morris for his encouragement, friendship, and scholarship; Subhana Ansari and Mahmoud Mostafa for their meticulous care in copy-editing; Lori Wood for thoughtful reading and comments.

Notes on Translation

In most cases we have attempted to transliterate Arabic words as they are pronounced. In quoted material, the spelling may vary according to the custom of the author. Throughout this book, references to the Qurʾān are in parentheses. These refer to the name of the *sūrah,* the *sūrah* number, and verses (*āyāt*). The first time the Prophet Muḥammad ﷺ is mentioned in a paragraph, his mention is followed by the calligraphic symbol for *ṣalla Allāhu ʿalayhi wa sallam,* "May the peace and blessings of Allāh be upon him." When Muḥammad's companions are mentioned, they are followed with the symbol for *raḍīallāhu ʿanhu* (may Allāh be pleased with him) or *raḍīallāhu ʿanha* (may Allāh be pleased with her). In material that is being quoted, we have used the symbols to replace these blessings, but have not added them if they were not present in the original text.

When quoting the Qurʾān or referring in the text to God, exalted is He, we have used the masculine pronoun. Please be aware that this is merely a limitation of language and that within the universe and understanding of the Qurʾān, God is without gender and far beyond any words or manner by which we might try to describe Him/Her. *Subḥān Allāhi Rabbil-ʿālamīn!*

Table of Contents

Acknowledgments v

Notes on Translation v

Table of Contents vii

Introduction: The Function of Language 1

What is a Human Being? ***Kabir Helminski*** 7

Primary Terms of Spiritual Psychology 9

The "I," Ego, Self, Anima, Psyche (*Nafs*) 10

The Heart (*Qalb*) 12

Spirit (*Rūḥ*) 13

The Servants of Spirit 13

The Structure of the Self 14

The Education of the Soul 16

Truth and Knowledge ***Prince Ghazi Bin Muhammad*** 19

(*AL-HAQĪQAH WAL MAʿRIFAH*) 19

Introduction 19

(1) What is Man? 20

(2) How Does Man Know? 23

2) a) The Body's Knowledge 23

2) b) The Soul's Knowledge 23

2) c) The Spirit's Knowledge 25

(3) The Nature of Knowledge 35

3) a) Truth 35

3) b) Knowledge 35

3) c) Doubt 36

3) d) Certainty 37

3) e) Faith 39

(4) The Types of Knowledge 42

4) a) The Different Types of Knowledge 42

4) b) Logic 43

4) c) The Islamic Sciences 45

4) d) Modern Western Sciences and Modern Technology 47

The Glossary 53
Terms in Arabic 53
ʿAbd 53
Ādāb 53
Ādam 54
Al-ʿAdl 54
ʿAdhāb 55
Ahl 55
Ahl aṣ-Ṣūffa 56
Aḥmad 56
Al-Akhfā 56
Al-Ākhirah 56
Akhlāq 56
Alast, Covenant of 57
ʿAlaq 57
Allāh 57
ʿAmal 58
Amānah 59
Amr 60
ʿAql 60
Al-ʿĀrif 61
ʿArsh 61
Asmāʿ ul-Ḥusnā 62
Āyah 63
Awliyāʿ 64
ʿAyn al-Yaqīn 64
Baqāʿ 65
Barakah 65
Barzakh 65
Baṣīrah 66
Al-Bāṭin 67
Bayān 67
Bidʿah 67
Ḍalāl 67
Dhāt 69
Dhawq 69
Dhikr 69

Dīn 74
*Du^c^ā^ɔ^* 75
Dunyā 75
Faqr 76
*Fanā^c^* 76
Fasād 76
Fayḍ 76
Fiqh 77
Fitnah 77
Fiṭrah 77
Furqān 78
Futuwwah 78
Ghaflah 78
Al-Ghafūr 78
Al-Ghaffār 78
Al-Ghayb 79
Ḥadīth 79
Al-Ḥajj 79
Al-Ḥakīm 79
Ḥalāl, Ḥarām 80
Hal and *Maqām* 80
Al-Ḥaqq 80
Ḥaqīqah 80
*Ḥayā^c^* 81
Al-Ḥayy 81
Ḥikmah 82
Himmah 82
Ḥirabāh 83
Hū 83
Ḥukm 83
^c^Ībādah 83
Iblīs 85
Iḥsān 85
Ijtihād 85
Ilhām 86
^c^Ilm 86

Īmān 89
Insān 91
Al-Insān al-Kāmil 91
Islām 92
Istikhāra 93
Jaḥīm 93
Jahannam and *Jannāh* 94
Jamal and *Jalāl* 95
Jihād 95
Kāfir 96
Kalām 98
Karīm 98
Khalīfah 98
Khuluq 99
Kufr 99
Kun 99
Malāᶜika 99
Maqām 99
Maẓhar 100
Minhāj 100
Mīzān 100
Muᶜmin 100
Murāqabah 101
Murīd 101
Murad 101
Mushrik 101
Nabī 101
Nafs 101
Niyyah 101
Qalb 101
Qiblah 101
Ar-Rabb 102
Rabita 102
Raḥmah 102
Ar-Raḥmān 103
Ar-Raḥīm 103
Rasūl 104

Ribā 104
Rūḥ 105
Saḥāba 105
Ṣalaḥa 105
Ṣalāh 105
Aṣ-Ṣamad 106
Sirr 106
Shahādah 106
Shahīd 106
Shaikh or *shaykh* 106
Shayṭān 107
Sharīʿah 107
Shirk 108
Shūrā 110
Ṣifāt 111
Sunnah 111
Tafakkur 112
Tanzīl 113
Tanzīh 113
Taqwā 113
Ṭarīqah 115
Tashbīḥ 115
Tawakkul 115
Tawbah 115
Tawḥīd 115
Taʾwīl 116
Umm 116
Ummī 116
Ummah 116
Wahm 117
Waḥy 117
Wajd 118
Wajh 118
Al-Wujūd 119
Yaqīn 119
Zakāh 120

Ẓulm 120
Terms in English **122**
Angel, *Malak* or *Mal'ak*, plural *Malā'ikah* 124
Appropriateness 124
Attainment 124
Awareness 124
Beauty 125
Beloved 125
Compassion and Mercy, *Raḥmān* and *Raḥīm* 125
Completion 126
Contentment, *Qanū*ᶜ 126
Contemplation 126
Consciousness 127
Discipline 127
Ecology 127
Effort 127
Ego, *Nafs* 128
Egoism 128
Elder 129
Emancipation 129
Epiphany 129
Essential Self 129
Essence 130
False Self 130
Freedom 132
Humbleness 132
Imaginal 132
Imagination 132
Intellect, ᶜ*Aql* 133
Interdependence 134
Knowing Heart 134
Knowledge, ᶜ*Ilm* 134
Leader 134
Love, *Ḥubb* 134
Lower Self 136
Maturity 136
Meditation, *Murāqabah* 136

Metaphysics 138
Mind 138
Mysticism, *Taṣawwuf* 138
Pharaoh 139
Personality 139
Prayer 140
Prophet, *Nabī, Rasūl* 140
Reality 140
Religion 140
Remembrance 140
Revelation, *Waḥy, Tanzil* 140
Self 140
Service, *Khidmah* 141
Sigh of Compassion, *Nafas ar-Raḥmān* 142
Sign 142
Sin 142
Sincerity, *Ikhlāṣ* 143
Soul 143
Spirit, *Rūḥ* 143
State, *Hal* 143
Station, *Maqām* 144
Submission, *Islām* 144
Supplication, *Du^c^ā* 144
Supraconscious 144
Thought, *Fikr* 144
Truth, *Al-Ḥaqq* 145
Universal Intellect, *^c^Aql-i Kull* 145
The Unseen, *Ghayb* 145
Will, *Irāda* 145
Wisdom, *Ḥikmah* 146
Witnessing, *Mushāhada* 146
Yearning, *Shawq* 147
Appendix A 151
The Arabic Root QWM *Jeremy Henzell-Thomas* 151
Some convergences with English words 151

Appendix B **155**
A Pedagogy for Exploring a Divine Name *Jeremy Henzell-Thomas* 155
Al-Quddūs 155
Educational implications 156
Bibliography **159**

Introduction
The Function of Language

The Book of Language is an exploration of the language we use to express the fundamental truths of the human condition. Foremost in importance are those terms found in the Holy Qurʾān that describe the human being and spiritual development.

This "glossary" has three principal purposes. The first is to explore the spiritual vocabulary of the Qurʾān. The second is to build a more precise spiritual vocabulary in the English language. The third is to shed some light on how terms in one language may be translated into another language—especially Arabic to English, and English to Arabic. All three of these tasks are interrelated and illuminate each other.

Unless we can define and clarify a language for the purpose of communicating the essential spiritual truths of our human situation, it will be difficult to understand one another and to communicate about matters of fundamental importance to our souls. Much confusion, argument, disagreement, and misunderstanding can be avoided by clarifying our terms. Beyond that we may be able to reach deeper levels of communication and understanding if we have a language for our inner experience.

Wittgenstein said: "The limit of my word is the limit of my world." The Roman poet and orator, Cicero, wrote two thousand years ago, "Before one discusses any subject whatsoever, one should first agree on terms." Terms and symbols are the subject and medium of thought. The critical importance of terminology is that words become premises, and conclusions always follow premises, at least in logical thought. In classical logic, problems start when one has either false premises or false words to express them.

Just as terms in the legal or scientific field require clear definition, so, too, in the field of human psychological and spiritual experience we need well defined terms. Fortunately, the basis for such a language already exists.

The Holy Qurʾān is believed to be a direct communication from God in the Arabic language. The explanatory power of its key terms is related both to how these terms are used in their various Qurʾānic contexts, as well as their etymological derivation from their Arabic root meanings. Both of these factors have contributed to making their meanings somewhat stable through time, unlike terms in English which are tied to no sacred reference point and undergo constant shifts of meaning with usage.

Nevertheless, although Qurʾānic Arabic has remained relatively stable in meaning over the centuries because it is determined by the usage of terms in this single text, the use of these same terms in vernacular languages such as Turkish, Persian, and Urdu can drift into other meanings and those new meanings can, in a sense, contaminate the understanding of the original Qurʾānic text. The shifting nature of meaning in other languages is therefore a obstacle to our understanding of the original Qurʾānic text.

Every field of knowledge requires its own specific vocabulary, a well-defined glossary for its own needs. English is a relatively undeveloped language for the expression of spiritual truths, especially when compared to certain languages like Sanskrit, Greek, Hebrew, or Arabic. These languages not only have a long history as vehicles for the expression of spiritual realities, they are also considered to be the recipients of revelation, by which we mean a direct communication from Divine Intelligence.

In order to be able to communicate with each other and to achieve a coherent knowledge, we would do well to have a spiritual vocabulary that is both precise and unified. To be unified means that each term in our glosary is related to the Whole, to the master truth of a coherent system, i.e., the Divine. To give one example, in the definition of "humbleness," for instance, we find a relationship between this single word and the master truth of spirituality: *The awareness of our dependence on God, and our interdependence and need for other human beings. We are not the originators of anything but the reflectors of the attributes of Spirit; all of our qualities, virtues, and capacities have their ultimate source in God, upon Whom we depend.*

Ideally, every word of our spiritual vocabulary should clarify and support other terms and remind us of the essential truths of a comprehensive knowledge. While it is true that the Arabic language, for instance, may have a precision, depth, and allusiveness that English lacks, we still have an obligation to use the English language as well as we can. This is made all the more urgent as English has become the most widely spoken language on our planet.

Finding corresponding terms between two or more languages can never be exact. A glossary which clarifies the meanings of corresponding terms, however, can bring them closer and infuse one or the other with greater meaning. "Repentance," for instance, has the root meaning to reflect on punishment (re-poena); the Islamic term for repentance, *tawbah,* however, has the more positive root meaning of turning in a new direction.

If we can succeed at clarifying the underlying issues of translating Arabic to English and vice versa, we will also contribute to the understanding between languages that have been deeply influenced by Islam (Turkish, Persian, Urdu, Swahili, Indonesian), on the one hand, and European and other languages, as well.

For the most part, the translation of the Qurʾān into European languages has been determined by the conventions of Biblical translation. This brings up two concerns: one is the choice to translate into a "religious" dialect, as if God has a different vocabulary and prefers words like "thou" and "verily." This sets sacred language apart from our human language, but unfortunately, to the ears of many, dresses God in the robes of an English Vicar. No such equivalent language style existed in Arabic at the time of its revelation. As sublime as the language of the Arabic Qur᾿ān is, not everyone believes its translation requires this kind of artificial support. This, however, is a relatively minor issue compared to our second concern: the more substantive issues at the level of meaning itself.

On the one hand, there should be some continuity of meaning and terms within the Abrahamic traditions of Judaism, Christianity, and Islām. On the other hand, since Islām understands itself to be a corrective to certain man-made distortions of religion that arose over the course of history, it should not be assumed that there is a one-to-one correspondence between terms such as "faith," "religion," or "sin," for example.

A prime example would be the common translations of the terms *muᶜmin* and *kāfir* as "believer" and "unbeliever," in which the essential Arabic meanings of *īmān* and *kufr* are only obscured. Believer and unbeliever suggest to the Western mentality an acceptance or rejection of a particular theology or institutional religion. But the Qur᾿ānic terms suggest a more fundamental disposition and much subtler notions of a human psychological state. *Īmān* connotes, all at once, being faithful, secure, and having verified the reality of the spiritual dimension. *Kufr*, on the other hand, connotes being in a state of denial, ingratitude, and a stubborn reluctance to face reality. If we allow these terms to become one-dimensional, to mean little more than the mere profession of doctrinal belief, or its lack, we have lost dimensions of meaning which are essential to our spiritual well-being. We have lost the meanings of *īmān* and *kufr*, themselves.

One of the first examples of mistranslation that set me upon this path of trying to understand the issues of translation was the case of the word *ᶜAlaq*. This word is used in the first *āyāts* revealed to Muḥammad ﷺ: *Read, in the name of your Sustainer who created, created the human being from ᶜalaq* (*Sūrah al-ᶜAlaq* 96:1-2). Unfortunately, too often it has been translated in a very unscientific way as "blood clot," which, for anyone acquainted with a minimum of biological science, brings discredit upon the revelation itself. If the Qur᾿ān is the word of God, cannot God give a better description of the origin of human life than from a clot? If we look into the Arabic word, however, we see that *ᶜalaqa* means establishing some sort of relationship, and ʿ*alaq* also describes anything that has a linking capacity. In this age of bio-engineering are we really going to maintain a translation of "clot" for ʿ*alaq*, or can we find something general enough and yet able to convey some of the scientific accuracy that is actually implied by the term? ʿ*alaq* could, for instance, be descriptive of DNA's double helix. It need not, however, be translated by something as specific as DNA, because as science develops, this understanding may be surpassed. The challenge is to find a translation that better embodies the meaning of some kind of substance that does not mislead us into unproductive areas of thought. A better solution would seem to be Muḥammad Asad's translation: "germ cell." This, at least, does not mislead and is more scientifically accurate. A somewhat long but more accurate and literal translation might be "an infinitesimal, clinging substance." But, unfortunately, that's eleven syllables in English to translate two in Arabic.

What, then, is the meaning of a word? Arabic words can usually be traced back to three-lettered roots, each associated with a family of meanings. Latin has a similar tendency to yield up many words from a single root: *sanctus* ("holy") produces in English, for instance, sanctuary (noun), sanctify (verb), and sanctified (adjective).

When interpreting the Qurʾān and its language we might keep certain principles in mind.

First, if we accept the Qurʾān as the word of God, we will take seriously its exact wording. In other words, we will consider that particular words are used, and that more than one level of meaning might be conveyed by a particular word. We explore the text open to all its linguistic possibilities, holding God to His word, so to speak.

Second, we can look to the root meaning of words. In what ways was the word used at the time it was revealed? For example, God is called *Al-Jabbār*, which is usually translated as the Compeller, the Irresistible. We might first think that God is being described as an overpowering force, but if we explore the various contexts in which the word was used, we find that it is also used to describe the mending of a broken bone; in other words, that irresistible process of healing that Life is endowed with. Here we glimpse the purely beneficent dimension of *Al-Jabbār*.

Third, we should realize the limits of etymological analysis, just as we would in another language. Because a word can mean something in a certain context does not mean that we can read that same meaning into another context. For example: the word "hard" in English can mean: 1. not easily dented. 2. demanding great physical or mental effort. 3. unemotional, as in "hard-hearted." 4. causing pain or discomfort. 5. containing much alcohol, as in "hard liquor." 6. shrewd, as in a "hard" customer. 7. stern, as in a "hard" master. 8. done with great force, as in a "hard" blow. Clearly, certain interpretations only apply to particular situations.

Fourth, we may look at the various contexts in which a word appears in the Qur᾽ān and in this way let the Qur᾽ān itself teach us. *Al-Furqān*, for instance, means "the criterion of discernment," and at the same time it is offered in certain contexts as a synonym for a Divine Revelation, including the °Injīl (Gospel) and the Tawrāh (Torah). This helps us to understand that the very purpose of revelation, itself, is to develop our capacities of discernment by offering objective criteria.

For anyone wishing to deepen the study begun in this book we would recommend studying the occurrence of key terminology as it appears in the Qur᾽ān. Kassis' "*A Concordance of the Qur᾽ān*" has proven to be a very valuable tool, but also the new edition of Muḥammad Asad's "*The Message of the Qur᾽ān*" has an excellent index that allows for the finding of terms in English, which can then be cross-referenced through the Arabic or Arabic transliteration. Those who can easily read Arabic will, of course, be able to do their own searches through various other resources and online.

Finally, we know very well what an enormous task we have undertaken and how this is only a modest beginning to a never-ending project. We hope that this may be an example to inspire others to reflect on the issues of sacred language, and to carry this kind of study much further in the future.

Kabir Helminski

What is a Human Being?

The structure of the self within an Islamic spiritual psychology

THIS ESSAY ATTEMPTS TO DESCRIBE AND CLARIFY the fundamental elements and structure of the human being. In a spiritual psychology, however, the human being is not viewed in isolation but in the context of a spiritual universe. The well-being and fulfillment of the human being cannot be separated from this larger reality.

Traditional Islamic spirituality provides a vocabulary that can help us to know and understand ourselves and our relationship to the Divine Being, Allah. From this vocabulary we can derive a sacred psychology that includes a model of the human being as well as a map of spiritual development.

To establish and clarify an appropriate vocabulary for understanding our human nature is a challenge that requires the cooperation of reason and revelation, the integration of human wisdom and divine guidance. If we can successfully present a true spiritual psychology, it will help to inform other areas of knowledge. This work will rest on a solid Qurʾānic foundation, and, at the same time, it should create a bridge toward contemporary psychological language and understanding.

No one who has studied the circumstances of the Qurʾān's revelation would deny that it proceeded from a deep level of inspiration, nor can one deny that it has its own inherent unity. This is part of its miracle: that the closer one looks, the more precision and order seem to reveal themselves.

Its terms are increasingly appreciated for their objective quality. If you gather together all the references to "heart" within the Qurʾān, for instance, you will see how they inform each other and suggest an objective and practical knowledge. The psychology of Islām, therefore, is not something formulated by the theorizing intellect; rather it is a unified body of knowledge whose source is this inspired text as it has been understood by generations of wise human beings.

The outcome of this knowledge and practice is humanizing and life-enhancing. The principles of spiritual development expressed in the Qurʾān stand as remarkable tools in purely practical psychological terms. For the believer, however, there is the faith that one's actions and intentions *here* will resonate forever in an eternal dimension and that our choices here have consequences far beyond our immediate earthly life.

Psychology means "knowledge of the soul (psyche)." While modern psychology and psychotherapies have shed some light on certain aspects of emotion, motivation, and personality formation, nevertheless, an objective science of the soul still proves to be elusive. Even the best contemporary psychologies are, to a great extent, a collection of subjective and culturally determined conjectures. There are dozens of theories of personality, theories of learning, and so on, but contemporary psychology does not offer a coherent understanding of the human being and the purpose of life. Insofar as they claim to be scientific, these theories are rudimentary experiments that hardly begin to fathom the most important issues of meaning and purpose in life.

Here we must face the central question that separates those who defend and maintain a purely secular reality from those who believe in the great tradition of revelation on this earth. The secular materialists believe that human beings can construct an effective and satisfactory knowledge of the human psyche from the ground up, so to speak. Freud and Marx are the outstanding examples of this mentality for the twentieth century. The failure of Marxism as a solution to social and economic injustice is hardly a matter of debate. The failure of Freudianism as a model for human psychological well-being, though less dramatic, is no less noteworthy. Such systems as these were not without their elements of insight and truth, nor were their discoveries and critiques entirely irrelevant. However, their failure was that they could not offer a satisfactory model of the highest purpose of human life.

What we are witnessing in the new millennium is a cultural collapse of modernism. "Modernism" had reduced existence to an impersonal scientific process. The human being was conceived as a biological machine functioning within an impersonal universe. Hopes for human well-being were placed in scientific methodologies that addressed only the material aspects of existence.

Much of the contemporary world and its academic and social institutions now refer to a so-called "post-modern" era, a time when all value systems, religious beliefs, and intellectual orientations are viewed as mere subjective human constructs. In other words, from the post-modern point of view all claims for ultimate "truth" are suspect.

Muslims, however, live in a different universe, though not necessarily one of pre-defined and pre-packaged "beliefs." The essential message of the Qurʾān is an encouragement to reflect on the signs of nature, to reason, and to open the heart to the Divine Presence. The Revelation offers certain propositions to humankind and asks that these be verified in our experience. Allāh, as Divine Intelligence, is guiding and educating human beings to the extent that they use their minds to reflect (*tafakkur*), use their intelligence (*ʿaql*), sustain remembrance (*dhikr*), and purify their own souls.

Primary Terms of Spiritual Psychology

The structure of the human individuality within an Islamic spiritual psychology can be understood through three primary elements: *nafs,* or ego-self; *qalb,* or heart; and *Rūḥ,* or Spirit. Together these form the human being.

The *nafs* is the self operating in the world, involved with actions and choices based on its own well-being, interests, and desires. The *nafs* faces insecurities, fears, and disappointments, as well as moments of happiness, pleasure, satisfaction, and peace. The *nafs* is the soul having an earthly experience.

There is another side of the human being, however, which is profoundly spiritual, able to access the divine qualities, knowing, luminous, conscious: *Rūḥ.*

Finally, there is *qalb*, the heart, the sensitive, knowing, feeling capacity of the human being. Athough in some human beings the heart may be hardened, diseased, contracted, or numb, when it is healthy and open, the heart is the meeting place of these two different sides of human nature, *nafs* and *Rūḥ*. Through the heart, the *nafs* receives energy, support, guidance, and inspiration from *Rūḥ*.

If the human being were visualized as a sphere, the ego would be like its surface, the heart would be its interior, and the Spirit would be its very center. The ego is the most superficial part of ourselves which, nevertheless, often vies for unquestioned control of our lives. The heart, as our interior, can be ignored and even denied. The Spirit, like a dimensionless point at the center of oneself, is like a portal to another dimension—the source of our life and consciousness.

In attempting to bring some clarity to these terms, we are faced with the problem that our English language uses them in vague, if not contradictory, ways. So we are compelled to create a spiritual glossary of our own.

The "I," Ego, Self, Anima, Psyche (*Nafs*)

Why must we use several English words to translate one Arabic word? The subject of the human "I" or self seems an elusive one. It is convenient that we have one word, *nafs*, in the Islamic vocabulary to convey the idea of a "self." The complexity and subtlety of the subject comes from the fact that the quality of the self, itself, can vary. We may experience our "I-ness" in very different ways, depending on factors like our "persona," the degree of the social mask we wear, our psychological defenses, our own state of self-awareness, and our willingness to reveal ourselves to others. It is common to say, for instance, that one person has a big ego, while another seems self-less. In each case we are talking about the identity, the sense of self that a person exhibits.

Nafs is what we most often experience as "I." People derive their sense of "I" from different sources. Some people, for instance, are completely "I"-dentified with their nationality, or their religion. Others are identified with and draw their sense of self and self-worth from their social status, how other people view them. Still others identify with their own deepest values and this identification will give them a stability of identity that allows them to survive the ups and downs of life.

The kind of education we are proposing, an education that includes the "vertical" dimension of spiritual education, will result in a continuing transformation of one's sense of "I." What we take to be our "I" today, we should not be so quick to believe is our real and truest "I."

Let us examine, for instance, this creature called "ego." The ego, if carefully observed, reveals itself to be a complex of psychological manifestations arising from the body and related to its pleasure and survival. If the body is hungry, the ego acts to satisfy the hunger. If some threat to life or well-being is perceived, the ego mobilizes what is necessary to escape or confront it. The ego, at its most basic level, is ruled primarily by fear and desire.

If a person experiences cruel treatment as a child, the ego that is formed may be primarily concerned with defending itself, or perhaps inflicting cruelty on others. If a person is criticized, belittled, and shamed, the ego may lack confidence, self esteem, and self worth. If a person receives a healthy amount of love and attention, while learning to be a considerate human being, such a person may come into the world with a relatively healthy, balanced, and integrated ego.

All too often, however, the ego has no limit to its desires, whether these are appetites of the body or of the personality. The ego has an intimate relationship not only with the body, but with the socialized personality as well. The personality is like a veneer on the ego. It disguises the ego's agendas and strategies and makes them more socially acceptable. Sometimes the more "education" a person has, the thicker is the "veneer" of personality.

The *nafs* (self) should be the receptive pole of the individual, assimilating what the active pole, Spirit, can give. When the self has become receptive to Spirit, it may be called the inspired self (*nafs al-mulhama*).

When the *nafs*, the ego, becomes the active pole, driving the individual with its incessant demands, then a human being is out of balance. The most disruptive and evil manifestation of the self is known as the commanding self (*nafs al-ammāra*). This kind of self manifests itself as ambition, self-importance, selfishness, rationalization, fantasy, delusion, self-righteousness, and aggression.

As we shall see, the self needs the purified heart (*qalb*) and the Spirit

(*Rūḥ*) to guide and inspire it in order that it might truly mature as a spiritual being. On the other hand, the spiritual part of ourselves also needs the basic energy of the self (*nafs*) to aspire toward spiritual development.

The optimal state of human well-being is when the self is in harmony with Spirit. This comes about when the self can follow the guidance of the heart, mobilizing the energy of desire in service of the heart, rather than trying to satisfy the demands of the selfish ego. Put another way, the self must be in submission to the heart which is guided directly by Spirit.

How shall we achieve this state of surrender? Traditional spiritual teachings propose ways, guidelines, and methods that essentially serve this one purpose: helping the self come into harmony with Spirit through the mediation of the heart.

The Heart (*Qalb*)

The heart may be experienced as the interior space within ourselves, which we know in a different way than through our normal thinking mind. The heart knows with a deep and empathic knowing, often accompanied by physical sensations as well. We talk about being heart-sick, or having a restless, wounded, or cold heart. We also talk about giving our heart to something.

The heart has the ability to sense the significance and value of things and events. Only the awakened heart can know the true dimensions of the spiritual universe we live in by experiencing all the subtleties the heart is capable of perceiving.

It is the midpoint of the individual person, between the ego self and Spirit. When it is healthy and awakened it receives all that Spirit has to give and transmits it to the individual self. The heart also includes many subtle faculties of perception.

On the other hand, if the heart becomes too dominated by the materialistic concerns of the ego, it becomes contracted and numb and no longer functions as a heart at all.

Spirit (*Rūḥ*)

Rūḥ, Spirit (*pneuma,* Active Intellect, *nous*), can be understood as the non-individual aspect of the human being which is continuous with Divine Being itself. It is described in the Qur'ān as an impulse or command from our Sustainer: *Qul: ir-Rūḥu min 'Amri Rabbī.* (*Sūrah Al-Isrā*ʿ 17:85)

Spirit is the essence of life itself. It is like a non-dimensional point that is linked to the realm of Divine Unity and has access to the realm of Attributes, the Divine Names. Spirit is the source that nourishes the heart. Inspiration is the word that suggests the influence of Spirit on the human being.

Spirit dignifies the human being above animals, and even above angels. It is what enables Ādam to know the names of things and thus to participate in the creative power of God. *We have honored the children of Ādam. . .* (*Sūrah Al-Isrā*ʿ 17:70)

The Servants of Spirit

Spirit's servants, or functions, include conscious presence, conscious will, and conscious love.

Conscious presence is that comprehensive state of awareness in which we can be aware of our thoughts, feelings, and actions. It exists on a level above these other functions—a level from which we can witness what goes on in our minds, feelings, and behaviors. It is a state that needs cultivation and development. Many aspects of modern life conspire to weaken it.

Conscious will is simply the ability to make a conscious choice, to have an intention. It implies a certain level of awareness and then it is up to our will-power to follow through with the intention or decision. Once again, we have relatively few opportunities to exercise this kind of will in modern life. Materialism, consumerism, and hedonism conspire to keep us acting unconsciously from mostly unexamined desires.

Conscious love is that better part of ourselves that can recognize and do what is right, regardless of self-interest, desire, or fear. Conscious love perceives and feels the unity of all life. The more conscious love we experience, the richer, deeper, and happier we are.

All three of these are essential aspects of Spirit which can enter the heart and transform the ego. Spirit has other important servants as well, including reason, reflection, wisdom, and conscience.

The individuality, the totality of the person, is the result of the relationship of these three: ego-self, heart, and Spirit.

The Structure of the Self

The human being can also be understood in terms of two fundamental axes. One axis we can call the conscious-unconscious axis. Another is the false self-essential self axis.

The four terms diagrammed below represent, in a necessarily simplified way, some fundamental dimensions of the human being. The movement from the false self to the essential self is a movement that increases awareness on the vertical axis of conscious and subconscious mind.

Conscious Mind
Ego, "I"
Personality
Intellect/Reason
Reflection
Awareness

False Self ⇨ ⇨ ⇨ ***Essential Self***

Subconscious Mind
Emotion
Heart
Intuition
Creativity
Wisdom

We begin with a sense of self, an "I," something we all experience.

Every time we say "I," that "I" is making some claim for itself: "I am happy today." "I am Fāṭima." "I am an American." What this experience is like varies enormously from person to person, from a contracted, separate self to an expanded, spiritualized Self. This "I", however, is a very small part of ourselves. It is only as much of ourselves as we are conscious of, or believe ourselves to be.

Beyond this "I" or conscious mind is a vast realm which can be called the subconscious. It might also be called the "supraconscious" if we want to emphasize that some of our higher impulses may originate from this realm, but for the sake of simplicity we shall use the familiar term "subconscious." Commonly, in conventional psychology, the subconscious mind is viewed as a kind of warehouse of buried memories, conditioning, complexes, drives, and obsessions. From a more spiritual perspective this subconscious is also the heart, the source of wisdom and subtle perceptions. It is infinite, at least compared to the conscious mind, and is spontaneously in communication with other minds, with mind-at-large, and with Spirit.

Any true education should help us to understand and make use of the relationship between the conscious mind and the subconscious mind. Our conscious sense of who we are is the fruit of the totality of our memories, attitudes, and beliefs at the subconscious level of mind, whereas the ideas we consciously hold in awareness, the impressions we take into ourselves, and what we allow to occupy our attention will be transferred to the subconscious mind and become a part of who we are.

When we know and are convinced of this, we will be in a better position to assume responsibility for our conscious mind. We will better understand how intention, positive thought, and prayer can affect our whole being positively, while negativity, anger, and fear can create a toxic state of mind.

The other polarity which needs clarification involves the false self and the essential self. The basic premise of this model is that the conscious mind is often identified with the false self, which is the product of fear and selfishness. We can free ourselves of this false self and through conscious *presence, will,* and *love* come to live from our essential self. Both these terms, false self and essential Self, are relative and not absolute. From the perspective of the essential self we feel our unity with everything through love and through the finer faculties of mind.

Where we identify on the false self and essential self continuum influences our experience of "I," as well as the condition of our subconscious mind. Clearly, someone whose life is ruled by vanity and greed and all the delusions they bring will have a different sense of self than someone who can remember his own mortality, his interdependence with the whole of life, and his dependence on God. The former will be enslaved to the tyranny of his own ego; the latter will experience an abundant and creative life, living from the essential self.

This could all be so simple, but for how long have we and generations before us made it so complicated? And yet we are created to know ourselves; we are created for this self-awareness; we are fully equipped for it. What could be more important than to know ourselves?

The Education of the Soul

Education as it is currently understood, particularly in the West, ignores the human soul, or essential reflective capacity at the heart of human beings. This reflective capacity is not some vague entity whose existence is a matter of speculation, but our fundamental "I," capable of intention (*niyyah*), conscious presence (*hudhur*), vigilance (*taqwā*), remembrance (*dhikr*), and faithfulness (*īmān*). This soul, or essential self, has been covered over by the superficiality of our thinking processes which are oriented toward the outer world rather than the development of our innate human capacities. Materialism and commercialism have conditioned many human beings to the extent that they are almost solely preoccupied with satisfying the artificial and random desires of the consumer world, rather than knowing and exploring their own inner capacities. Today we are in great need of a form of education that would contribute to the awakening of the soul. Such forms of training have existed in other eras and cultures and have been available to those with the yearning to awaken from the sleep of their limited conditioning and know the potential latent in the human being.

The education of the soul, or the "vertical" dimension of education, is different from the education of the personality or the intellect. Conventional education is all about acquiring external knowledge and "making something of ourselves" in the outer world. The education of the soul involves not only knowledge, but the realization of a quality of being which is our deeper nature, and which includes conscious presence, conscious will, and conscious love. The education of the soul is the spiritual development of the inner human being through successive stages in which the quality of "I-ness" becomes more and more illuminated by Spirit (*Rūḥ*). It is a process of the self becoming more fully human and more fully spiritual at the same time.

What is most characteristically human may not be guaranteed to us by our species or by our culture, but is given only in potential. A person must *work* in order to become human. What quality makes us most distinctly human? What is most human in us is something more than the role we play in society, and more than the conditioning (whether for good or bad) of our culture. The human being has been shaped by the Creative Spirit and brought forth as a witness who could keep the covenant offered to it and fulfill the task which is the purpose of its life. The human being is the conscious caretaker and representative (*khalīfah*) of the Creative Spirit on the earth—with the potential for conscious presence, will, creativity, mercy, and love. By establishing the right relationship among the three essential elements of our being—self, heart, and spirit—we can fulfill the task of being completely human.

Truth and Knowledge
(*Al-Haqīqah wal Ma^crifah*)

Prince Ghazi Bin Muhammad

In the Name of God, the Compassionate, the Merciful
And above every possessor of knowledge, there is one with more knowledge.
(Sūrah Yūsuf 12:76)

Introduction

THE BRANCH OF PHILOSOPHY concerned with knowledge, truth and *how we know* is known in English as *epistemology*. It is the first and most important of all the branches of philosophy and is the basis of all forms of knowledge and science. Thus it precedes all the natural sciences: understanding the nature of knowledge itself obviously comes before having knowledge of particular things. It is not an inherently easy subject, but in what follows we will try to summarize it without over-simplification.

However, even before we discuss *epistemology* we must first ask *what we are—what man as such is*—for it is illogical to want to know something existing *within* man without first knowing what man himself is. And evidently knowledge is something existing within man.

(1) What is Man?

The Human Being (*al-insān*) is comprised of three major elements: a spirit (*rūḥ*), a soul (*nafs*), and a body (*jism*). Each of these exists in its own plane or world and yet they are all connected.

1) a) The Body

Everyone knows, feels, and uses the body. It is the living, physical, and animal part of man. It is the part of man that breathes, eats, and moves, and enables him (or her) to exist in the Physical Universe (*ᶜĀlam ash-Shahādah,* the universe of witnessing). It is also the mortal part of man: that part of man which can become ill, grow old, and die. Indeed, physical death is nothing other than destruction of the body and its separation from the soul and spirit of man, which nevertheless remain intact:

> *Until, when death cometh unto one of them, he saith: My Lord! Send me back that I may do right in that which I have left behind. But nay! It is but a word that he speaketh, and behind them is an Isthmus (Barzakh) until the day when they are raised. (Sūrah al-Muᶜminūn 23:99-100)*

1) b) The Soul

The soul (*nafs*) of the human being is really man himself, his or her particular personality, what makes him an individual. It is also, as the great ancient philosopher Plato (427-347 BC) said[1], immortal (*khālidah*): it survives man's physical death. It is thus superior to the body, just as the world in which it exists (called the *barzakh*, as in the verse just quoted) is superior to the Physical World where bodies exist. Many scholars have described the soul's relationship to the body as analogous to the relationship of a king to his kingdom, or a captain to his ship. It controls the body, makes its decisions, thinks for it, and stands in relationship to it like a kind of "inner witness."

The soul has three major parts: "the soul that inciteth unto evil" (*an-nafs al-ʾammārah bis-sūu*) (*Sūrah Yūsuf* 12:53), "the soul that blames" (*an-*

---

[1] Plato, *Phaedrus*, 245.

nafs al-lawwāmah) (*Sūrah al-Qiyāmah* 75:2), and "the soul at peace" (*an-nafs al-muṭma'innah*) (*Sūrah al-Fajr* 89:27). "The soul that inciteth unto evil" and "the soul that blames" are constantly struggling within man to lead toward evil and good, respectively. Plato likens their struggle to two horses fighting to take a chariot in different directions:

> As to the soul's immortality, then, we have said enough, but as to its nature there is this that must be said. . . . Let it be likened to the union of powers in a team of winged steeds and their charioteer. . . . [I]t is a pair of steeds that the charioteer controls; moreover, one of them is noble and good, and of good stock, while the other has the opposite character, and his stock is opposite. Hence the task of our charioteer is a difficult and troublesome business.[2]

Now the 'charioteer' here is an allegory for "the soul at peace," except the "soul at peace" does not become "at peace" and *return to its Lord* (*Sūrah al-Fajr* 89:28) until "the soul that blames" manages to overcome "the soul that inciteth unto evil," or as Plato says, until "the wicked horse abandons his lustful ways[3]" and conforms to the reproaches of "the good horse" (which is nowadays known as the conscience [*ḍāmir*]). It is only then that the virtues, which are naturally in the soul, can manifest themselves freely, and that the soul can *Enter My Paradise*... (*Sūrah al-Fajr* 89:29).

Even modern psychology acknowledges that the soul has three parts which check and balance each other. The Austrian psychologist Sigmund Freud (1856-1939) called them the "id," the "ego," and the "superego." These correspond roughly to Plato's "bad horse," "good steed," and "charioteer," respectively, except that Freud, being an atheist, did not ever imagine that the "id" could come to be truly "at peace" or could "*return to its Lord*."

1) c) The Spirit

The word 'spirit' (*rūḥ*) has two meanings: the first simply means "the

---

2 Plato, *Phaedrus*, 246 a-b.

3 Plato, *Phaedrus*, 255.

life" within a body. The second, which is the one we are using here, refers to the spirit which is the inner witness of the soul and the body taken together. This spirit is the Divine breath within man. As the Holy Qur'ān says:

> *Then He fashioned him [man] and breathed into him of His spirit; and appointed for you hearing and sight and hearts. Small thanks give ye! (Sūrah as-Sajdah* 32:9*)*

The spirit is superior to the soul (and of course the body) because it is not just immortal but free from individual personality and restrictions. Equally, its world, the *ʿĀlam al-Malakut,* is superior to the world that contains the souls, for it is in the Hand of God and contains the essences of all things in the two worlds below it:

> *Therefore glory be to Him in Whose hand is the dominion (malakūt) of all things! Unto Him ye will be brought back. (Sūrah Yā Sīn* 36:82*)*

Beyond this, however, little can be said about it because it is infinite and it comes from God:

> *They will ask you about the spirit. Say: The Spirit is by command of my Lord, and of knowledge ye have been vouchsafed but little. (Sūrah al-Isrāʿ* 17:85*)*

Finally it should be said that, although it might seem strange that man has, in a certain sense, two subjectivities (the individual soul and the spirit which is beyond the individual personality), it is also a necessity. Otherwise how could every man be "I" by himself, and yet still be men like other men? And how could the soul really know itself but for the spirit that is beyond it; for as Plato says: "the eye cannot see itself." Moreover, the fact that there is both a soul and a spirit also explains why, in the Holy Qur'ān, God promises every single pious person two paradises:

> *But for him who feareth the station of his Lord there are two paradises. (Sūrah ar-Raḥmān 55:46)*

(2) How Does Man Know?

Each of man's 'parts' knows, or can know, the realities existing on its own plane through epistemological faculties naturally found within itself. These are the three main sources of knowledge.

2) a) The Body's Knowledge

The body, which is a physical entity, knows physical realities through its physical senses, and then "communicates" them to the soul. Its sees through the eyes, hears through the ears, smells through the nose, tastes through the mouth, and feels through the skin; and all of these are forms of knowledge of the physical world. This form of knowledge is often called "sense perception."

2) b) The Soul's Knowledge

> *By the sun and its brightness,*
> *And the moon when it followeth him,*
> *And the day when it revealeth him,*
> *And the night when it enshroudeth him,*
> *and the heaven and Him who built it,*
> *And the earth and Him who spread it,*
> *And a soul and Him who perfected it,*
> *And inspired it [with conscience of] what is wrong for it*
> *and [what is] right for it.*
> *He is indeed successful who purifies it,*
> *And he indeed is a failure who corrupteth it.*
> (*Sūrah ash-Shams* 91:1–10)

The soul is a subtle (*laṭīf* or *khafiy*) entity. In addition to the information relayed to it by the body and the physical senses (through the mind and its "physical seat," the brain) the soul knows in three primary subtle ways. These are the intelligence, the will, and the sentiment, which are called the "cognitive," "behavioral," and "affective" systems, respectively, by modern psychology. The intelligence is made for comprehending the true, the will is made for freedom of choice, and sentiment is made for loving the good and the beautiful. Put in another way, we could say that man's soul knows through *understanding* the truth, through *willing* the good, and through virtuous *feeling*. True knowledge is thus not just mental comprehension, but rather feeling and willing, for to truly understand what is good, beautiful, and noble necessarily means to love it and to want it.

In fact, it is precisely these three faculties that set man apart from animals and explain why he is God's representative (*khalīfah*) on earth (God says in the Holy Qur'ān, *Sūrah al-Baqarah* 2:30: *Lo! I am about to place a khalīfah upon the earth*...). For on earth only man has an intelligence capable of true objectivity and of knowing the truth in its fullness. Only man has a will capable of total concentration, of complete freedom, and thus of absolute self-sacrifice. And only man has sentiment capable of sincere love, true goodness, and altruistic virtue. Man is born with these faculties in his soul, for these are essentially Divine gifts for *Verily God created Ādam in His own image*[4], but they are only "unfolded" gradually as a child grows up: sentiment develops with consciousness almost inseparably from birth; the will and the intelligence start to develop shortly thereafter and become unfolded (if still inexperienced and unlearned) before puberty.

Each of the soul's three main epistemological faculties can then be divided into certain "modes": the will can be positive or negative, combative or ascetic, vigilant or self-disciplined, aggressive or cowardly. Sentiment can be active, passive, loving, peaceful, passionate, contented, confidant, grateful, hopeful, or happy. The intelligence, however, has four major modes: reason, which is objective; intuition, which is subjective; imagination, which is prospective; and memory, which is retrospective. On a different plane, these "modes" can be further subdivided into different "functions" and "aptitudes": as regards "functions," which are more essential, we can distinguish first between discernment (*tamayyuz*) and contemplation (*ta'ammul*), and then between analysis and synthesis. As regards 'aptitudes', we can distinguish between an intelligence that is theoretical and another that is practical, and then between one that is spontaneous and another that is reactive; or again, between an intelligence that is constructive and another that is critical. Finally, mention should be

---

[4] *Musnad* Ibn Ḥanbal, 2: 244, 251, 315. 323 etc.; *Ṣaḥīḥ Bukhārī, Kitāb Al-Isti'thān*, 1; *Ṣaḥīḥ Muslim, Kitāb Al-Birr* 115, *et al.*

made of the linguistic faculty, which extends the intelligence outside of itself and permits communication.

Incidentally, it is these different faculties, modes, functions and aptitudes that explain why one student is naturally better at a given subject (but not at all of them) than another: in each person they develop slightly differently, leading to different gifts in different subjects. Also, since real knowledge involves loving and willing something, it is also clear that students who really like a subject and want to work at it, will do better than those who do not.

2) c) The Spirit's Knowledge

2) c) i) Revelation

The highest form of knowledge is that which accompanies Revelation (*waḥy* or *tanzil*), for it comes from outside of man—from God Himself, who is Omniscient. It is the very Word of God. It is meant for all mankind or for a whole nation (*ummah*), but it only comes to Prophets and Messengers, (and is, in fact, what makes them Prophets or Messengers):

> *He hath revealed unto thee [O Muḥammad] the Scripture with truth, confirming that which was [revealed] before it, even as He revealed the Torah and the Gospel.* (*Sūrah Āl ʿImrān* 3:3)

> *Lo! We inspire thee as We inspired Noah and the Prophets after him, as We inspired Abraham and Ishmael and Isaac and Jacob and the tribes, and Jesus and Job and Jonah and Aaron and Solomon, and we imparted unto David the Psalms; and messengers We have mentioned unto thee before and Messengers We have not mentioned unto thee; and God spake directly unto Moses. (Sūrah an-Nisāʿ 4:163-164)*

The Qurʾān tells us that, with the death of the Prophet Muḥammad ﷺ, the Seal of the Prophets, the door of Revelation was closed, and there will be no more Revelation until the second coming of the Prophet Jesus عليه السلام.

2) c) ii) Inspiration

Below the knowledge from Revelation is the knowledge that comes from the spirit (*rūḥ*) and whose source is also ultimately *from God* or from God's Presence (*ladun*):

> *[A]nd I know from God that which ye know not. (Sūrah Yūsuf* 12:86*)*

> *Then found they one of Our slaves, unto whom We had given mercy from Us, and had taught him knowledge from Our presence. (Sūrah al-Kahf* 18:65*)*

This knowledge is called Inspiration (*ilhām*)[5]. It is said to be infallible, direct knowledge of things as they truly are, in their own realities, unlike knowledge which comes from the soul of a person:

> *And I did it not upon my own command. Such is the interpretation wherewith thou couldst not bear. (Sūrah al-Kahf* 18:82*)*

The Holy Qur'ān says:

> *Is he who payeth adoration in the watches of the night, prostrate and standing, bewaring of the Hereafter and hoping for the Mercy of his Lord…? Say: Are those who know equal to those who do not know? But only men of understanding will pay heed. (Sūrah az-Zumar* 39:9*)*

2) c) iii) The Heart

In discussing spiritual knowledge mention must be made of the heart. In fact, the word "heart" has two meanings: one is the physical heart that pumps blood around the body. The second, which is the one that concerns us in this context, is the subtle heart that is the means by which spiritual knowledge is communicated to the soul.[6] For this reason it has sometimes been described as a bridge between the soul and the

---

[5] It is also often called "unveiling" (*kashf*).

[6] Hence the *ḥadīth*: "Hearts are God's vessels on earth, and most beloved unto Him are the finest and clearest of them." (Al-Hakim At-Tirmidhī, *Nawadir al-Usul fi Maʿrifat Aḥadīth ar-Rasūl*, IV, 34). See also ʾAḥmad bin Ḥanbal's *Kitāb az-Zuhd*.

spirit, to which only the pure have access, all other people having a kind of 'rust' over it which prevents them from accessing it. The Holy Qur'ān says:

> *They have hearts, but do not understand with them.* (*Sūrah al-Aʿrāf* 7:179)
>
> *It is not the eyes that are blind, but blind are the hearts within the breasts.* (*Sūrah al-Ḥajj* 22:46)
>
> *What, do they not ponder the Qurʿān? Or is it that there are locks on their hearts?* (*Sūrah Muḥammad* 47:24)
>
> *They would trick God and the faithful, and only themselves they deceive, but they are not aware. In their hearts is a sickness.* (*Sūrah al-Baqarah* 2:9–10)
>
> *No indeed; but what they were earning has rusted their hearts.* (*Sūrah al-Muṭaffifīn* 83:14)
>
> *He has written faith upon their hearts.* (*Sūrah al-Mujādalah* 58:22)
>
> *It is He who sent down tranquility into the hearts of the believers, so that they might add faith to their faith.* (*Sūrah al-Fatḥ* 48:4)
>
> *Then, even after that, your hearts were hardened and became as rocks, or worse than rocks, for hardness. For indeed there are rocks out from which rivers gush, and indeed there are rocks which split asunder so that water floweth from them. And indeed there are rocks which fall down for fear of God. God is not unaware of what ye do.* (*Sūrah al-Baqarah* 2:75)

All of this also explains why the Prophet ﷺ said: "The intelligence of the *kāfir* (the denier, conventionally called 'the unbeliever') is half the intelligence of the *muʿmin* (the person of faith, conventionally called 'the believer')."[7]

[7] *Sunan* An-Nasā'ī, *Al-Qasamah*, 38.

Since only believers can have access to the heart and to spiritual knowledge, and since unbelievers can have no access to this higher kind of knowledge, it can be said that the intelligence of unbelievers is only half that of believers, no matter how clever they are in the remaining half.

Immanuel Kant and his Denial of the Heart and of Spiritual Knowledge

The reality of the heart and of spiritual knowledge was well known all over the ancient world and in the West. Even in the Gospel, Jesus عليه السلام is reported to have said:

> And Jesus answered him, The first of all commandments is, hear O Israel, the Lord our God is one Lord; And thou shalt love the Lord thy God with all thy heart, and with all thy soul, and with all thy understanding, and with all thy strength: this is the first commandment. And the second commandment is like, namely this, Thou shalt love thy neighbour as thyself. There is none other commandment greater than these.[8]

(Note here also that the basic faculties of the soul are the same as those described above: the *heart,* the *soul, love,* the *will*—which is the source of *strength*—and the *intelligence* or *comprehension.*)

Despite this widespread traditional knowledge of the spiritual faculty, there have always been people who have doubted the reality of the heart—or have accepted it without being fully convinced—for the simple reason that they themselves never had any experience of it, nor personally knew anyone who has (indeed, few people ever do). However, the first person not only to deny the soul's existence but to try to prove philosophically that it could not possibly exist was the German philosopher Immanuel Kant (1724-1804). In his *Critique of Pure Reason* (1781) and his *Prolegomena to Any Future Metaphysics* (1783), Kant argued that knowledge of things in themselves (which he called "pure reason") was logically self-contradictory and humanly impossible and thus that metaphysics, which is the formal doctrine of this kind of knowledge, was merely empty specula-

[8] *The Gospel according to St. Mark* 12:29-31 (see also *Deuteronomy* 6:5 and *Matthew* 22:37-9).

tion. Of course Kant was right in one sense: "direct" or "pure" knowledge is impossible on the level of the soul, because although the soul is quite adequate to knowing truths in an indirect sense, it can never fully free itself of its preconceptions and its individual perspective.

Consider a chair. Any chair. Everyone knows what a chair is, but no one sees it exactly from the same angle. And no one sees it from all angles at once. And when one sees it, one does not, merely through seeing it, immediately know all its properties or its age or its history. One does not know its inherent nature. It could be just about to collapse, but one may not know that simply by looking at it. Moreover, one does not know the chair directly in itself, but rather through an image one has of it in the soul transmitted through the eyesight, the memory, or the imagination. But that image is sufficient to enable us to go and sit on it, or to pick it up, or to tell someone we have just seen a chair, or to know that the chair is not a table or a ladder or even a bunch of grapes. Thus the soul has real and true knowledge but not pure or direct knowledge.

From the perspective of Islamic metaphysics, the spirit does mysteriously have pure knowledge, because this knowledge ultimately comes from God, albeit it exists on a different level than that of the soul. Kant's mistake was to assume that just because he did not have such knowledge, or did not know anyone who had it, then no one *could* have it. His argument was like that of someone who had never been to China, nor known anyone who had ever been to China, suddenly saying not only that China does not exist, but actually trying to prove that it does not exist. Unfortunately, however, after Kant, belief in the existence of spiritual knowledge among philosophers all over the world weakened and continues to weaken among philosophers—and even among believers—to this day.

2) c) iv) The Intellect (*al-ᶜAql*)

There is, however, one kind of spiritual knowledge that is accessible to all men. This is knowledge of the Intellect. First, however, it should be pointed out that the word *ᶜaql* in Arabic now has at least three different meanings. The first quite simply means the mind (*adh-dhihn*) which, itself, is a general term indicating unspecifically the general intelligence, consciousness, and comprehension of a soul. This is the sense of the term used in the *ḥadīth* quoted above (that "the intelligence of the unbeliever is half the intelligence of the believer"). The second means specifically the faculty of logic in the soul, as mentioned earlier and discussed later. The word is often used by philosophers in this particular sense. The third, which is the sense we are concerned with here, means a ray of knowledge or intelligence that comes ultimately from the spirit, through the heart down through the depths of the soul even to the very body. If we compare light to knowledge, the sun to the spirit, the moon to the soul, and the earth to the body, then the Intellect can be compared to a ray of light in the night that comes from the sun, hits the moon, is reflected off it, and finally is projected onto the earth.

When this ray is at the level of the heart, then we simply identify it with the heart itself, and when it is at the level of the soul, we identify it above all with intuition, which we have already mentioned as providing us "subjective knowledge." It is this intuition which provides believers with mysterious perception (*baṣīrah*) of things and insight (*firāsa*) into people. The Prophet ﷺ said:

Beware the insight of the believer for he sees through God's light.[9]

It is also this intuition that enables us to contemplate things by holding them in our mind without thinking rationally about them, but only by contemplating (*taʿammul* or *tadabbur*) them passively, and then suddenly to understand them. This is the sense of the term *ʿaqila* that the Holy Book uses in verses like the following:

> *Lo! In the creation of the heavens and the earth, and the difference of night and day, and the ships that run upon the sea with that which is of use to men, and the water which God sendeth down from the sky, thereby reviving the earth after its death, and dispersing all kinds of beast therein, and in the ordinance of the winds, and the clouds obedient between heaven and earth, are signs for people who use their intellects (yaʿqilūn).* (*Sūrah al-Baqarah* 2:164)

Finally, when the intellect is "at the same level as" the body it produces animal instinct. But what is instinct? To understand this properly

---

[9] *Sunan* At-Tirmidhī, *Kitāb Tafsīr Al-Qurʿān*, *Tafsīr Sūrah al-Ḥijr* (15:6).

we must ask the following questions: when one drives a car, or merely walks down the street, having a serious conversation, who is talking? Then who is driving? How do we dodge when something is thrown at us? And how do migratory birds fly alone, sometimes for the first time, all the way across the world to a specific place where they meet other birds? How do newborn crocodiles (and other animals) that are abandoned by their parents have the skills to survive?

Let us consider the first question first: if the soul is concentrating the intelligence and the will on the conversation, then it is obviously not these faculties that are driving the car or operating the legs. Certainly, it is not the spirit or the heart, for spiritual knowledge is of a different nature, as we have said. It is not the body, for the body in itself cannot think. As for what is nowadays called the subconscious, these are merely the tendencies and the desires of the ego and thus part of the soul, which is otherwise engaged, and which anyway has no active capacity to think other than through the intelligence. Thus it is something else. In fact, this something else is none other than the intellect, albeit in a fragmented and distant form, and it is this that explains all the questions asked above. In fact it is through this intellect that God ultimately gives each thing—animals and humans alike—the innate knowledge it needs to survive and to be fully itself, and although we commonly call it animal instinct, it is actually often miraculous. The Holy Qur'ān reminds us that God inspires even animals:

> *And thy Lord inspired the bee, saying: Choose thou habitations in the hills and in the trees and in that which they thatch. Then eat of all fruits, and follow the ways of thy Lord, made smooth for thee.... (Sūrah an-Naḥl* 16:68-69*)*

2) c) v) Visionary Dreams (*ar-Ru'yā aṣ-Ṣāliḥa*)

We must not forget to mention visionary dreams in this section because they are seen not only by Prophets, like the Prophet Abraham (in *Sūrah aṣ-Ṣaffāt* 37:102), the Prophet Joseph (in *Sūrah Yūsuf*, 12:4), and the Prophet Muḥammad himself ﷺ (in *Sūrah al-Fatḥ*, 48:27; *Sūrah al-Anfāl*, 8:43), but also by ordinary believers, from prisoners in jail (*Sūrah Yūsuf*, 12:36) to kings (*Sūrah Yūsuf*, 12:43). The Prophet ﷺ said: "The visionary dream of the truly believing Muslim is one forty-sixth of prophecy."[10]

This means that visionary dreams can provide real knowledge to believers. Muslims faced with an apparently irresolvable question can pray for a dream using the method known as *istikhāra* (see Glossary of Arabic terms) to ask God what to do. (This however requires certain conditions: one must believe; one must have a genuine need and not merely a desire to have a vision; one must have exhausted all other means of resolving the question including reflection, consultation, prayer and supplication; and one must be resolved to submit to the answer whatever it is).

It should be noted, however, that obviously not all dreams (*manāmat*) are visions: the vast majority of dreams are confused, "psychic dreams" (*ʾaḍghāthu ʾaḥlām*, in *Sūrah Yūsuf* 12:44) which are merely a kind of mental "playback" and "information processing," often including the day's memories, imaginings, emotions, physical sensations, associations, and so on.

The Prophet ﷺ said: "Visions are from God, dreams are from the devil."[11] Indeed, visions are distinguished from ordinary dreams by their clarity and intelligibility; by their occurring at "blessed moments" (such as at the time of *fajr*, just before sunrise) often with the person awake towards the end of the vision; by their revealing blessed elements from outside of worldly time and space such as Prophets and Angels (the Prophet ﷺ said: "Whoever sees me in a dream has really seen me"[12]); by the "imprint" that they leave, which often lasts right through the day; and by their usually coming for a specific merciful purpose such as to give good news, to encourage, to comfort and console, or to warn of a danger. The Prophet ﷺ said: "Nothing remains of prophecy except glad tidings (*mubashshirat*). They said what are glad tidings? He said: True Visions."[13]

---

[10] *Ṣaḥīḥ* Bukhārī, *Kitāb At-Taʿbīr*, 4.

[11] *Ṣaḥīḥ* Bukhārī, *Kitāb At-Taʿbīr*, 3.

[12] *Ṣaḥīḥ* Bukhārī, *Kitāb At-Taʿbīr*, 10.

[13] *Ṣaḥīḥ* Bukhārī, *Kitāb At-Taʿbīr*, 5. It should be noted, incidentally, that visions are symbolic in form and that one needs to know how to interpret them. The best book on this subject is *Muntakhib al-Kalām fi Tafsīr al-Ahlam* by Ibn Sirin (33-110 A.H.; 653-729 C.E.)

2) d) Summary of the Three Main Sources of Knowledge

In one of the most famous passages in Western literature and philosophy, Plato tells the story of certain prisoners in a cave as a parable for man's condition.

> Compare the effect of knowledge and the lack of it upon our human nature to a situation like this: imagine men to be living in an underground cave-like dwelling place, which has a way up to the light along its whole width, but the entrance is a long way up. The people have been there since childhood, with their necks and legs in fetters, so that they remain in the same place and can only see ahead of them, as their bonds prevent them from turning their heads. Light is provided, burning some way behind and above them. Between the fire and the prisoners, some way behind them and on a higher ground, there is a path across the cave, and along this a low wall has been built, like a screen at a puppet show in front of the performers who show their puppets above it. . . . See then also men carrying along that wall so that they overtop it, all kinds of artifacts, statues of men, reproductions of animals in stone or wood fashioned in all sorts of ways, and, as is likely, some of the carriers are talking, and some are silent.
>
> These prisoners are like us. . . . Do you think, in the first place, that such men could see anything of themselves and each other except the shadows which the fire casts upon the wall of the cave in front of them? . . . If they could converse with one another, do you not think that they would consider these shadows to be the real things? . . .
>
> Consider then what deliverance from their bonds and the curing of their ignorance would be if something like this naturally happened to them. Whenever one of them was freed [he would first turn around and see the puppets and then, after climbing up the path of the cave to the real world] would see objects in the sky . . . the light of the stars, the moon and the light of the sun during the day. . . .
>
> The men below have praise and honours from each other, and prizes for the man who saw the most clearly the shadows that passed before them, and who could best remember which usually came earlier and which later, and which came together, and thus could most ably prophesy the future. . . .
>
> If this man went down to the cave again and . . . had to contend again with those who had remained prisoners . . . would he not be ridiculed? Would it not be said that he returned from his upward journey with his eyesight spoiled, and that it was not worthwhile even to attempt to travel

> upward? As for the man who tried to free them and lead them upward, if they could somehow lay their hands on him and kill him, they would do so.
>
> The realm of the visible should be compared to the prison dwelling, and the fire inside it to the power of the physical sun [in real life]. If you interpret the upward journey and the contemplation of things above as the journey . . . to the spiritual world, you will grasp what I mean. . . .[14]

Thus, from the Islamic perspective, we have three levels or sources of knowledge in ascending order of reality: the knowledge of the body or the physical senses, and these are the shadows of the puppets; the knowledge of the soul (when it is virtuous and thinking correctly, and has *certainty*, as will shortly be discussed) and these are the puppets themselves; and spiritual knowledge, and this is the knowledge of the 'real things' of the 'real world', the moon, the stars and so on. The men who are chained and believe nothing but the shadows and set great store by them to the extent that they want to kill anyone who disturbs them, these are the materialistic people who believe only what their physical senses transmit to them and who, with their prizes and honours, are merely playing an empty game. God says in the Holy Qur'ān:

> *Know that the life of this world is only play, and idle talk, and pageantry, and boasting among you, and rivalry in respect of wealth and children....* (*Sūrah al-Ḥadīd* 57:20)

The people who have seen the real things and try and warn the prisoners, these are the Prophets and Messengers, and the hostility they meet is like the hostility of most people towards their own prophets that we find expressed in the Qur'ān. And finally, the cave is this physical world from which only faith in the messages of the Prophets frees us and gives us real knowledge!

---

[14] Plato, *The Republic*, Book VII, 514-517.

(3) The Nature of Knowledge

3) a) Truth

Truth is absolute by nature. This means that something which is true is so completely and utterly, and that its reality exists independently of all knowledge or perception except God's. In other words, something which is true is so, no matter what anybody or everybody says or thinks about it, and conversely, merely thinking about it cannot affect it in any way. This is because *truth comes from God's own nature*:

> *That is because God is the Truth! Lo! He quickeneth the dead, and lo! He is Able to do all things. (Sūrah al-Ḥajj* 22:6*)*

Herein lies the reason why lying is such an offense to God: it is an affront to His Nature which is the Truth. Thus God also says:

> *Confound not truth with falsehood, nor knowingly conceal the truth. (Sūrah al-Baqarah* 2:42*)*

3) b) Knowledge

Knowledge is by definition knowledge of truths. Knowledge that is not ultimately true is not knowledge, but rather merely opinion, belief, conviction, judgment, information, theory, or illusion. In fact, most of what passes for knowledge nowadays, most of what we think we know, even most of what is taught in universities, is merely opinion, beliefs, judgments, convictions, theories, and illusions. We cannot be certain whether these are in fact true.

So how can one know if what one thinks is the truth or not? *How do we know that we know?* This question has been much discussed by modern philosophers. But the answer to it is simple: objective truth *by its own nature* imposes, in various degrees, subjective certainty in the soul, provided of course the soul is sane and *in its innately pure state* (*fiṭrah*). For, as mentioned earlier, God created man in His own image, and thus capable of knowledge (since He is the Knower). Indeed, the Qur'ān contains the prayer:

Oh Lord, increase me in knowledge! (*Sūrah Ṭā Hā* 20:114)

This of course *implies* that man *is* capable of knowledge.

3) c) Doubt

Before discussing certainty, we will first consider its opposite, doubt, in order to understand what certainty is not. Since the earliest times in human history, there have been those who have managed to doubt various things, and even those who have managed to doubt everything:

> *And they say: We will not put our faith in thee till thou cause a spring to gush forth from the earth for us. Or thou have a garden of date palms and grapes, and cause rivers to gush forth therein abundantly; Or thou cause the heaven to fall upon us piecemeal, as thou hast pretended, or bring God and the angels as a warrant; [or] Thou have a house of gold; or thou ascend up into heaven, and even then we will not believe in thine ascension till thou bring down for us a book that we can read. Say: My Lord be glorified! Am I naught save a mortal messenger?* (*Sūrah al-Isrā᾽* 17:90-93)

The earliest formal school of philosophy based essentially on doubt was that of the Ancient Greek *Skeptics* (which started about 80 BCE). The *Skeptics* basically argued that, since information was affected by perspective and appearances, one should suspend all judgments on truth, and that only then could one be intellectually honest and have peace of mind.

One thousand five hundred years later, the French Philosopher René Descartes (1596-1650) went even further and proposed that the only way to attain certain knowledge is by doubting everything until one found something that could not be doubted. This was called "doubt as [philosophical] method," and with it he went so far as to doubt the reality of the world and to entertain the possibility that it was an illusion or a hoax played on him by another being. Finally, however, he concluded that the one certainty he had and upon which could construct his views about the world was that he knew that he *thought*, even while he was doubting, and this meant that he did after all exist. His famous maxim "I think, therefore I am" ("*Cogito ergo sum*" in Latin) was for him the starting point of philosophy, certainty, and even all knowledge.

This prepared the ground for the British philosopher David Hume (1711-1776) to take doubt and its philosophy—skepticism—to its ultimate and most extreme conclusion, solipsism. Hume asserted that one cannot know anything—or even know if anything actually exists—outside of our minds, because all we have are perceptions which are themselves filtered, altered, and arranged by our minds. In other words, meaning and the illusion of reality is created by our minds, as they are in ordinary dreams, so that true knowledge and reality do not exist.

Many other philosophers have pointed out that the problem with these suggestions is that they are both hypocritical and self-contradictory. They say they are hypocritical because all the doubters, skeptics, and solipsists (including Descartes and Hume themselves) would eat when they were hungry and drink when they were thirsty, without doubting that they were hungry or thirsty; they would all certainly have run if a bull chased them, and screamed if a dog bit them, and none of them would have said or did say: "I doubt the world exists, therefore I am going to allow myself to be burnt like the Prophet Abraham, or to be sacrificed, like his son, who had the courage of their convictions." They say they are self-contradictory because, after all, these philosophers did bother to write and tell us what they thought, and so obviously they believed enough in the existence of other people to do that! *Thus doubt is merely lack of certainty and does not in itself prove anything.*

3) d) Certainty

We mentioned earlier that objective truth *by its own nature* imposes subjective certainty, in various degrees, in the soul, provided, of course, the soul is sane and *in its innately pure state* (*fiṭrah*). This means that when one objectively and disinterestedly has an unshakeable and undoubtable feeling of certainty about something—and not merely passionate conviction based on what we want or what we fear—this usually means that thing is true. It goes without saying, however, that the person has to be intelligent, sane, and virtuous (which is the sanity of the immortal soul which will have to face the Final Judgment).

This is easier to understand as regards the body than as regards the soul, so let us consider the body first, by way of example. When one feels something, or tastes something, or sees or smells or hears something, this is usually because they are there: the sensory impulses work mechanically and cannot be faked in a healthy body, even if they can later be misinterpreted by the mind. We say "in a healthy body" because it is in theory always possible to "rewire" the mind so that you "see" sound waves and "hears" colour waves, and it is certainly true that people with amputated limbs sometimes "feel" those limbs.

In the soul, the intelligence works in much the same way: the certainty of the purified soul is an indicator of the truth. We also acknowledge that there are sub-normal states in which a person is not capable of the same kind of objective certainty (for obviously the insane can hallucinate, the mentally impaired can misunderstand or misjudge, and the old can simply be senile). God says:

> *And God created you, then causeth you to die, and among you is he who is brought back to the most abject stage of life, so that he knoweth nothing after having had knowledge. Lo! God is Knower, Powerful.* (*Sūrah an-Naḥl* 16:70)

The two other main faculties of the soul, the will and sentiment, also work in a similar fashion, provided, as mentioned above, that the soul is virtuous and in its primordial state—which in fact only the souls of the Prophets and the righteous (*ṣāliḥin*) are *fully*—for this is sanity and health of sentiment and will. Thus unlike people of bad character and even ordinary, fallible people who can love and will evil things, when a prophet wills something, it is because that thing is good, and when he loves something, it is because that thing is noble and beautiful. Indeed, this alone is true love and true good will:

> *Yet of mankind are some who take unto themselves rivals to God, loving them like that which is due to God, but those who believe are stauncher in their love for God ....* (*Sūrah al-Baqarah* 2:165)

★★★

Now there are three main degrees of certainty: *ʿilm al-yaqīn* (see

Sūrah at-Takāthur 102:5), *ᶜayn al-yaqīn* (see *Sūrah at-Takāthur* 102:7) *and ḥaqq al-yaqīn* (see *Sūrah al-Wāqiᶜah* 56:95). *ᶜIlm al-yaqīn* (*Sūrah at-Takāthur* 102:5) is to know something that is true with certainty, but only with certainty of the soul, and not with certainty that reaches down through the depths of the soul to the heart:

> *And when Abraham said: My Lord! Show me how Thou giveth life to the dead, He said: Dost thou not believe? Abraham said: Yea, but in order that my heart may be at ease....* (*Sūrah al-Baqarah* 2:260)

ᶜAyn al-yaqīn (*Sūrah at-Takāthur* 102:7) is the next step, and it is when the soul begins to see with its "inner" eye, which is none other than the heart. Finally, *ḥaqq al-yaqīn* (*Sūrah al-Wāqiᶜah* 56:95; *Sūrah al-Ḥāqqah* 69:51) is when a person is completely and utterly consumed by the truth, just like those who have passed on to the next world (*al-ākhirah*, which is *dār al-ḥaqq*, the realm of the Real, precisely):

> *And lo! We know that some among you will deny it. And lo! it is an anguish for the disbelievers. And lo! It is the absolute truth. So glorify the name of thy Tremendous Lord.* (*Sūrah al-Ḥāqqah* 69: 49-52)

This is the ultimate certainty. Needless to say, it, and even *ᶜayn al-yaqīn*, usually apply only to the absolute Truth (and by extension to fundamental principles and religious truths), not to ordinary facts.

3) e) Faith

Once again here, one word has slightly different meanings in different contexts: faith (*al-īmān*) in the more general sense is to know that God exists and to trust in Him. In a particular sense it is a specific degree of this knowledge:

> One day the Messenger of God ﷺ declared before the public that a man came to him and said: Messenger of God, what is *Īmān*? Upon this he replied: That you affirm your faith in God, His angels, His Books, His Meeting, His Messengers, and that you affirm the Resurrection hereafter. He (again) said: Messenger of God, what is *Islām*?

He said: *Islām* is that you worship God and do not associate anything with Him and you establish obligatory prayer and you pay *Zakāt* and that you observe the fast of Ramaḍān. He again said: Messenger of God, what is *Iḥsān*? He replied: That you worship God as if you see Him, for if you do not see Him, yet He sees you.... The Messenger of God remarked: He (the questioner) was Gabriel, and he came to teach people their religion.[15]

There are thus three degrees of religion (*dīn*): *Islām*, *Īmān* and *Iḥsān*, and they represent, in a certain sense, the three degrees of certainty mentioned in the previous section, only with respect to the religion of *Islām*. The first degree, *Islām*, is, as the words suggests, to accept and obey God, without profound belief, whilst the second degree (which is the particular sense of the word *Īmān*, as mentioned above) is belief which goes beyond the intelligence down into the heart:

The Arabs of the desert say: We have faith. Say thou: faith ye have not, but say "we submit," for faith hath not entered your hearts. And if ye obey God and his Messenger, He will in no wise withhold from you your need in what you do. Lo! God is Forgiving, Merciful. (*Sūrah al-Ḥujurāt* 49:14)

The last degree, *Iḥsān*, corresponds to *ḥaqq al-yaqīn* in the sense that in it the worshipper (*ᶜabd*) is completely overwhelmed and consumed as one would be if one actually saw God:

And when Moses came to Our appointed tryst and his Lord had spoken to him, he said: My Lord! Show me that I may gaze upon Thee. He said: Thou wilt not see Me, but gaze upon the mountain! If it stands still in its place then thou wilt see Me. And when his Lord revealed His glory to the mountain He sent it crashing down. And Moses fell down senseless.... (*Sūrah al-Aᶜrāf* 7:143)

It remains to be said about faith that it increases and decreases, for God says:

And that the faithful may increase in faith... (*Sūrah al-Muddaththir* 74:31)

---

[15] *Ṣaḥīḥ* Muslim, *Kitāb Al-Īmān*, 2.

And it increases or decreases depending upon man's actions (depending on whether they are sins or good deeds), for the heart is like a lamp, sin is like a rust on that lamp, good deeds are like the polish for the "rust" of sins, and faith is the brightness of that lamp; the Prophet ﷺ said:

> There are four kinds of hearts: a bright heart in which there is a shining lamp; a dark, covered heart with a lock on its cover; an inverted or relapsing heart; and a thin heart. As for the bright heart it is the heart of the believer whose brightness comes from his [or her] light. As for the dark heart, it is the heart of the unbeliever. As for the inverted heart, it is the heart of a hypocrite who knows and then denies. As for the thin heart, it is the heart in which there is both faith and hypocrisy; faith in such a heart is like a plant which pure water causes to grow, and hypocrisy in such a heart is like an ulcer in which there are pus and blood, so that whichever the heart is fed most by dominates it in the end.[16]

And:

> If the servant commits a sin a black spot forms on his heart, and if he changes, repents and asks for forgiveness his heart is cleansed. But if he [the servant] relapses, it returns until it dominates the heart, and it is the rust that God mentioned: *Nay, but that which they have earned is rust upon their hearts.* (*Sūrah al-Muṭaffifīn* 83:14)[17]

And God says:

> *If We will, We can smite them for their sins and seal their hearts so that they hear not.* (*Sūrah al-Aʿrāf* 7:102)

And, by contrast:

---

[16] *Musnad* Ibn Ḥanbal, *Ḥadīth Abū Saʿīd al-Hathri*, 147 / 11113.

[17] *Sunan* At-Tirmidhī, *Kitāb Tafsīr Al-Qurʾān, Tafsīr Sūrah al-Muṭaffifīn* (83:14); no. 3334.

Lo! those who ward off evil, when a glamour from the devil troubleth them, they do but remember, and behold they are seers. (*Sūrah al-Aʿrāf* 7:201)

From these examples we see how certain unbelievers can have very developed intelligences in certain areas, and even be geniuses: for faith does not depend solely upon the intelligence, but rather upon the state of a person's soul and their previous actions throughout life. Thus one can be very intelligent (as regards certain things) and at the same time be an unbeliever, or conversely one can be very simple and yet have great faith. Thus, in order to strengthen one's faith, one should simply pray, do good deeds, and avoid evil, and not merely debate about religion: and certainly no amount of talk, no matter how learned or sophisticated, will make an evil person good, or give an evil person faith.

(4) The Types of Knowledge

4) a) The Different Types of Knowledge

It can be said that there are three primary types of knowledge. The first kind, which we may call "higher knowledge," comes from faith and religion and is rooted in the heart and the spirit. It is the only kind of knowledge that gives *ʿayn al-yaqīn* and *ḥaqq al-yaqīn*, but since we have already discussed it sufficiently, we will discuss it no further here. The second kind we may call "definite knowledge," because it is based upon knowledge that has its roots in God's own Nature or in Revelation; this kind of knowledge gives *ʿilm al-yaqīn* (but only that). It includes the principles of mathematics (or at least arithmetic, which is rooted in unity of the number one and thus in the Divine Unity which it reflects), logic and the certainties or inevitabilities based in Revelation or in the nature of creation, like death (the Holy Qurʾān says: *Every soul shall taste of death.... Sūrah Āl ʿImrān* 3:185) and the progress of time. The third kind of knowledge we may call "empirical knowledge," but strictly speaking it is not knowledge at all, for it is inherently uncertain—it may or may not be true; it is ultimately impossible to tell which—and it is the basis of all the modern natural sciences, and certainly of all modern technology. In what follows, we will briefly discuss logic as an example of "definite knowledge"; the Islamic natural sciences as knowledge that is "definite" in principle, but which nevertheless engage in speculation based upon "empirical" data, and Modern Western "knowledge"—or rather *theories*—as "knowledge" that is entirely "empirical" and speculative in nature.

4) b) Logic

All of logic is based on two simple chief laws, and these chief laws are based on the Divine Nature of the Truth. These two laws are the *Law of Contradiction* and the *Law of the Excluded Middle*. The *Law of Contradiction* says that a proposition *cannot be* both true *and* false at the same time and in the same respect, and that something cannot both be and not be, or have a quality and not have it, at the same time and in the same respect. The *Law of the Excluded Middle* says that a proposition *must* either be true *or* false, and that something must either be or not be, and either have a particular quality or not have it. Now the *Law of Contradiction* is true because it asserts the absoluteness of truth—that something either is or is not—and thus reflects the Absoluteness of God (for truth comes from God, as we have seen). The *Law of the Excluded Middle* is true because it asserts the infinitude of truth—that there are no other possibilities other than something either being or not being—and thus reflects the Infinitude of God.

Let us give examples: as regards propositions, we may say that the proposition "I am in Jordan" is either true or false (according to the *Law of Contradiction*), and that there are no other possibilities other than its being true or false (according to the *Law of the Excluded Middle*). As regards being (*wujūd*) and qualities (*ṣifāt*), we may say that you cannot both be here *and* not be here (according to the *Law of Contradiction*), and that you *must* either be here or not be here (according to the *Law of the Excluded Middle*). It should be noted, however, that there are some terms that are *inherently not clearly defined* (for example, baldness) so that initially the two laws may seem not to work (for example, one could not say that a person is either bald or not bald, because balding people are in between the two), but in actual fact the laws are still true, it is just that the initial terms mean more than one thing or contain internal contradictions.

Moreover, even the laws of logic cannot be applied to propositions or ideas that do not make sense in the first place or are inherently self-contradictory.

Now these two laws may sound obvious and unremarkable (for we are all used to them without knowing them formally) but together they are the foundation of *syllogism* and most of the other methods of logic, including analogy. (A *syllogism* is when two premises are used together to form a conclusion. For example: *Fulan* is a man. All men must die eventually. Therefore *Fulan* must die eventually.) And logic itself is the basis of rational thought, and thus of the operation of the rational intelligence itself. Hence these two laws are of the greatest possible importance for knowledge.

It should be noted, however, that logic is only a tool for rational thought and not a science containing any information in itself, nor even a part of the intelligence. It is impartial in itself and depends entirely upon the initial premises to which it is applied for its conclusions. In this sense it is like a washing machine: it moves around what is put in, without adding anything to it of itself, but manages to clarify it before it comes out. It is not opposed to religion, as some people have imagined, but rather is a neutral instrument that can be used by religion or against religion. However, as we have said, its laws only work because they reflect the Divine Nature and so in that sense logic supports religion. Likewise, logic can either seem to support or undermine empirical science, depending on the initial premises of the argument.

The father of logic, the man who first formulated its principles and formalized its study, was the great ancient Greek philosopher, Aristotle (384-322 BCE). Aristotle was a student of Plato and the personal tutor of Alexander the Great of Macedon.[18] Like Plato, Aristotle believed that the soul was immortal, that God was One, and that God created everything in existence, but unlike Plato he did not bother to use Ancient Greek mythology as symbols for his ideas, and expressed himself through philosophical expositions rather than through dialogues. He called his writings on logic *The Organon* (which means "the tool," for that is how he

---

[18] Many commentators have said Alexander is none other than *Dhu'l-Qarnayn* in *Sūrah al-Kahf.*

saw logic), and he also founded and began the study of many of the natural sciences. Between Aristotle and Plato there is no science or field of study that they did not found or address—and no major question they did not ask, if not answer—from cosmology to biology, from politics to botany, from physics to philosophy to linguistics. They are considered the fathers of philosophy and of the sciences, to such an extent that it has been said that all subsequent philosophy is mere commentaries on their works.

4) c) The Islamic Sciences

From the start, Islām encouraged the acquisition of scientific knowledge. The Prophet ﷺ said:

The search for knowledge is incumbent upon every Muslim.[19]

This quest for knowledge was considered one of the most meritorious activities in life. The Prophet ﷺ also said:

> When a man dies all his acts are cut off from him, except three: recurring charity, or knowledge which benefits people, or a pious child who prays for him.[20]

Even worldly and empirical knowledge was not discouraged, although the Prophet ﷺ admitted that this was not his own specialty or mission when he said to the people of Medina:

> You are more learned in the affairs of your world.[21]

Thus various different kinds of learning developed and flourished under Islamic civilization in an unprecedented way. As Prince Charles, the Prince of Wales, says:

---

[19] *Sunan* Ibn Mājah, *Muqaddimah*, #17.

[20] *Ṣaḥīḥ* Muslim, *Kitāb Al-Wasiyyah,*19.

[21] *Ṣaḥīḥ* Muslim, *Kitāb Al-Fadail,* no. 2361.

> The medieval Islamic world, from Central Asia to the shores of the Atlantic, was a world where scholars and men of learning flourished. But because [the West has] tended to see Islam as the enemy, as an alien culture, society, and system of belief, [it has] tended to ignore or erase its great relevance to its own history. For example, we have underestimated the importance of 800 years of Islamic society and culture in Spain between the 8th and 15th centuries. The contribution of Muslim Spain to the preservation of classical learning during the Dark Ages, and the first flowerings of the Renaissance has long been recognized. But Islamic Spain was much more then a mere larder where Hellenistic knowledge was kept for later consumption by the emerging modern Western world. Not only did Muslim Spain gather and preserve the intellectual content of ancient Greek and Roman civilization, it also interpreted and expanded upon that civilization, and made a vital contribution of its own in so many fields of human endeavor—in science, astronomy, mathematics, algebra (itself an Arabic word), law, history, medicine, pharmacology, optics, agriculture, architecture, theology, music. Ibn Rushd and Ibn Ẓuhr, like their counterparts Ibn Sīnā and Abū Bakr ar-Rāzī in the East, contributed to the study and practice of medicine in ways which Europe benefited from for centuries afterwards.[22]

For all this learning, however, the Islamic Sciences, even when they incorporated theories based upon empirical observation, were distinguished by four important distinct features stemming from Islamic principles:

(1) They were generally undertaken with an attitude of piety, or spiritual conscientiousness (*taqwā*), with one of three motives: either the sheer love of knowledge, or for the sake of better knowing God's Creation—and through Creation, the "Ways" (*sunan*) and Nature of God—or for the benefit of mankind. If there were direct worldly profit from this knowledge to be had, then this was merely an added benefit.

(2) They never viewed the world or their sciences as cut off from God or the unseen world or even the Angels, but rather always remembered that God created the world, sustained it, and could change its course of events whenever He pleased. Thus the "miraculous" was part

[22] H.R.H. The Prince of Wales, "Islam and the West," A lecture given in the Sheldonian Theatre, Oxford, on 27 October 1993, pp.17-18.

and parcel of the world, and all worldly knowledge was slotted into a greater cosmological view of creation which started with God Himself and ended with the physical world.

(3) They always viewed man in his theomorphic dignity as God's Representative on earth (*khalīfat Allāh fil-ʾarḍ*), and not as some accident of biology or some statistic on an economic chart. Therefore the physical sciences did not pretend to be able to determine all of his behaviour or to reveal all of his secrets. Each human being possessed free will and thus remained an object of respect and value.

(4) Islamic scientists, like Ibn Sīnā for example, did not pretend to know through their logical powers only, but rather used to read the Qurʾān as the ultimate source of all certain knowledge (*ʿilm al-yaqīn*)—and pray for guidance and intuition, and pray for a "personal oracle" (*istikhara*)—so that there would be grace (*tawfīq*; *barakāt*) and truth in their knowledge.

All of this meant in practice that the Islamic Sciences—the sciences under Islām—did not produce knowledge that was based on false principles or that was in the long run harmful to man in this world or the next. Indeed the Prophet ﷺ had said:

> I seek refuge in God from a knowledge which does not benefit.[23]

Consequently, although the Islamic Sciences, through their preservation of ancient Greek knowledge, prefigured and led to the Modern Western Sciences as a matter of historical fact, they nevertheless were based on profoundly different principles from what was to follow.

4) d) Modern Western Sciences and Modern Technology

Before discussing the modern sciences and modern technology we should first say that for approximately 6000 years before 1800 CE, technology had not changed very much in the world's "high civilizations": that is to say that Ancient Egypt and Ancient Sumer over 6000 years ago already had everything from fire to the wheel; cities and states; massive

---

[23] *Ṣaḥīḥ* Muslim, *Kitāb Al-Dhikr*, 73.

construction (witness the pyramids) and fortresses; armies with catapaults, archery, and cavalry; metal mining; boats, navigation, fishing, and sailing; international trade and commerce; domesticated animals; farming, agricultural surpluses, and irrigation; writing and long-distance communication; bureaucracy and law courts; medicine and hygiene. Of course, as civilizations rose and fell again in various places according to natural cycles, their repositories of technical and scientific knowledge (or parts of them) were often lost and then (much later perhaps) gradually rediscovered again, but it is significant that the French Emperor Napoleon's armies in 1800 marched across the world at exactly the same speed (or, if anything, slower) as did those of Alexander the Great over 2000 years earlier.

Some time around the sixteenth century, as the faith of Europeans in Christianity, for various reasons, began to weaken, there arose a movement to study the natural world in itself, divorced from religion and higher principles, and based entirely upon making physical experiments, noting their results, and inventing theories using logic, analogy, and trial and error to try to explain them. The principles (or lack of them) of this secular movement were first formally formulated by the Englishman Francis Bacon (1561-1626), who also for the first time started to spread the idea that history, and in particular the history of science, was not cyclical as the scriptures (including the Holy Qur'ān) suggested, but rather a story of linear "progress" from the "worse" to the "better," from the "backwards" and "simple" to the "forward" and "complex."

The results of this "new science" were at first slow, as people and society took time to change, but by the end of the nineteenth century they had led to technologies which created an "industrial revolution" in Britain and some other Western countries. These countries developed electricity, photography, telegraph, trains and railways, factories, machines and mass production, steam-powered ships, and heavy weaponry. Moreover they had used these economic, military, communication, and transportational advantages to conquer at least three quarters of the rest of the world. By 1950 these technological inventions included radio, telephone, film, television, cars, planes, atom bombs, rockets, submarines, and huge discoveries in every conceivable scientific discipline, especially physics, energy production, agriculture, and medicine. By the end of the twentieth century they included computers, space flight, the internet, robots, super-conductors, genetic engineering, and satellite communication. These inventions themselves gave rise to a secular Western popular culture which followed them all over the world into every remaining traditional culture, eliminating many traditional ways of life such as nomadism and other subsistence life-styles. They also flooded the entire earth's population with such products as Western clothes, Coca-Cola and fast food, pop music, Hollywood films, Western sports, and with what is worse, a dependency on them. Thus in 200 years the world went through far more changes than it had for the 6000 years before that, or perhaps even since the creation of man. And it is still continuing to change at an ever-faster rate. All of this is due to the technologies that are the fruits of modern Western science.

Despite such spectacularly successful products, it could not be said that Western science was in itself *ʿilm al-yaqīn*, because, as we have said, it was not based on any certain principles or higher forms of knowledge. Rather, these experiments were financed by nation states, large corporations, or wealthy individuals seeking not the general good, or knowledge and truth, but rather primarily monetary gain and worldly power.

The development of Western science was based on theories constructed around the results of experiments based upon trial and error in much the same way as if one found 100 points that could be joined in a straight line and one made the assumption that a straight line was responsible for these hundred points. This sounds very reasonable, and is usually true. Were it not usually true, modern science could never have invented technologies that function so successfully. However, it is not *always* true. And it is not *necessarily* true: for nature is complex and there is no reason why after a hundred points in a straight line—or even a thousand—a pattern should not start doing something else, and start zig-zagging, for example.

Let us consider a historical example to illustrate this. The Englishman Isaac Newton (1642-1727) is universally considered to be the father of modern science. Among other things, he discovered or formulated differential and integral calculus (in mathematics) and the universal laws of motion, the most famous of these being the Law of Gravity. For more than two hundred years in Europe, people believed in Newton's Laws as if they were divinely revealed, and they were taught in every scientific institute in Europe as certain truth. The Laws were used (among other things) to predict very precisely the movements of the planets in the sky. However, by the beginning of the twentieth century, as more accurate telescopes started to be built, it was noticed that Newton's laws were incorrect with respect to the planet Mercury's motions, by something like one degree every 100 years (in other words, by something real, but in practice not noticeable). This led to a complete reconsideration of Newton's Laws which, as it turned out, did not hold true for things that were either very large (the size of planets) or very small (the size of atoms). Thus it can be seen there cannot be absolute *certainty* (*ᶜilm al-yaqīn*) about every modern scientific theory, despite empirical evidence that seems to prove them time and time again.

So are modern sciences and their fruits, modern technology, a good thing or a bad thing for mankind? In their favour we can say that they have saved billions of lives (through their medicines and through improved agriculture which have enabled the earth to support billions more people). They have also made life in general longer, healthier, wealthier, cleaner, more comfortable, easier, less painful, freer, and more amusing for the majority of people in the world. And they have made travel, transport, communication, and access to information incomparably quicker and easier.

Against them we can say that they have not made life safer or happier. Modern technologies have also killed millions of people (in wars and through modern weaponry). They have made it easier for some nations to conquer other nations. They have destroyed the majority of traditional cultures and ways of life, and are replacing them more and more with one shallow and secular popular culture where the most important things are money, material goods, and physical gratification. They have moved the majority of people from the countryside to cramped lodging in huge cities, and overwhelmed them with constant change, turmoil, noise, ugliness, confusion, unnecessary commercial products, and machines, making them feel small, lost, and insignificant.

It would be difficult to fully calculate the effects of modern technology on human life, but, among the effects that we can observe, they have impacted much of what previously gave meaning to life, such as worship, religion, family, nature, honour, love, and friendship. They have confused man and have tried to strip him of his free will with biological, chemical, and psychological theories that purport to make conclusive statements about what a human being is and claim to be able to predict his behaviour, despite generally being accompanied by an ethic of democracy which teaches that the most important human value is freedom. The unexpected ramifications of technologies seem to have increased the rates of divorce, social discontent, drug-taking, alcoholism, and crime all over the world. Through the effects of modern technologies the earth has been overpopulated, nature plundered, many natural habitats and species of life eliminated, and the environment polluted, so that it is now not clear if life on earth is sustainable in the long term. Weapons of mass destruction could at any time be used to destroy everybody and everything on earth. Finally, and perhaps worst of all, our technologies, governed primarily by economic necessities and the profit-motive, disconnected from a sense of what makes a human-being human, have not made people better or more virtuous, but if anything they have contributed to making them less virtuous and more distracted.

It is thus not clear on balance whether more good than bad has been achieved by the great power—if not the great truth—of modern science. One thing that is clear, however, is that it is now too late to turn the clock back and make science's inventions disappear. It is equally clear that nations that do not keep up with modern science and technology do not have the wealth or the might to defend themselves from the oppression of nations that do. Thus learning modern science and acquiring modern technology is, if not an inherently good thing, certainly a necessity to survive, and in that sense a duty for all.

Wa Allāhu ʿalam; wal-ḥamdu Lillāhi waḥdahu.
And God alone, all praise be to Him, truly knows.

The Glossary

Definition of a definition: A definition is a statement of what a thing is. It has to cover all kindred aspects of what is being defined, and should be free from all aspects which don't agree with it. In other words, a definition is a statement that should include all the "friends" of the defined and exclude all its "antagonists." Furthermore, a definition, like a lens, helps us to see the clear outlines of what is being defined. Finally, a definition can situate a word in a context of coherent meaning and show its relationship to other key terms within that greater structure of meaning.

Terms in Arabic

These are terms whose meanings are either central to understanding the Qurʾān or have acquired an important meaning in the tradition of Islamic spirituality. They are offered to clarify their etymological origins and Qurʾānic contexts and thus create a richer understanding of their usage.

ᶜAbd: عبد The servant and worshipper. *ᶜIbada*, from which *ᶜabd* is derived, suggests worshipping, serving, and knowing, all at the same time. The true servant of Allāh, *ᶜabdullāh*, is the one who knows Allāh and therefore can truly worship and serve Him. *I created jinn and humans only to worship Me* (*Sūrah adh-Dhāriyāt* 51:56).

Ādāb: أدب Courtesy, appropriate behavior;. In our context it is a subtle discipline of mind and body that expresses humility, respect, patience, and sensitivity.

Although Islamic education is often defined as *tarbiyah*—a "nurtuing" process—Al-Attas prefers to regard it as *tāʾdib,* a word related

ing" process—Al-Attas prefers to regard it as *tā'dib*, a word related to *ādāb*. He defines this term in its true sense (before its restriction and debasement of meaning to "a context revolving around cultural refinement and social etiquette") as "discipline of body, mind, and soul" which enables us to recognise and acknowledge our "*proper place in the human order*" in relation to our selves, our family, and our community. This order is "arranged hierarchically in degrees (*darajāt*) of excellence based on the Qur'ānic criteria of intelligence, knowledge, and virtue (*iḥsān*)." In this sense, *ādāb* is "the reflection of wisdom (*ḥikmah*)" and "the evidence (*mashhad*) of justice (*ᶜadl*).... Within the dual nature of man's own self, the *ādāb* of his lower animal soul *(an-nafs al-ḥayawāniyyah)* is to recognise and acknowledge its subordinate position in relation to his higher rational soul (*an-nafs an-nāṭiqah*)."

Ādam: آدم The first human being, who stands for all human beings. The significant quality of *Ādam*, or the human being, is that he has been bestowed with the knowledge of the divine names (*Sūrah al-Baqarah* 2:33), and that all the Angels, *Malā'ika*, were asked to bow down before him (*Sūrah al-Baqarah* 2:34). The story need not be understood literally to pertain to a specific person or pair of historical human beings; rather, this is the story of humanity itself, and *Ādam* is its representative.

It is widely believed that *Ādam*, understood as the first human created by Allāh, (whose story is narrated in the Qur'ān regarding his exit from *Jannāh*) was also the first Prophet, or *Rasūl*. This, however, is not mentioned in any verse of the Qur'ān, nor is the name of Eve or *Ḥawwā'* mentioned in the Qur'ān.

Al-ᶜAdl: العدل The Just, one of the beautiful names of Allāh. At the heart of Islamic understanding is this Qur'ānic verse, *wa tamaat kalimatu Rabbika ṣidqan wa ᶜadlān*, "And the Word of your Lord is fulfilled and perfected in truth and in justice." (*Sūrah al-Anᶜām* 6:115)

ᶜAdl (Justice) comes from the Arabic verb ᶜadala, which is usually translated as "to proportion," "to create in symmetry," or "to be equitable." A sense of justice comes from viewing life's situations from the divine perspective beyond personal prejudice. God addresses the Prophet David 🖼, *Behold, We have made thee a vicegerent on earth: judge, then, between men with justice, and do not follow vain desire, lest it lead thee astray from the path of God.* (Sūrah Ṣād 38:26) In other words we are not to allow subjective opinion to influence our sense of justice.

A second very important point derives from the notion that God's Mercy has precedence over His Wrath. Therefore, Mercy is an essential aspect of Justice. The faithful are often reminded that if they wish Mercy from their Lord, they must show mercy. Another hadith says: "God gives a reward for gentleness which He will never give for harshness."

In actual fact we are faced with the dilemmas of justice throughout our lives: to what extent do we strive for justice for others and ourselves, and to what extent do we bear with patience what may seem to be injustices done to us? The spiritual virtue of resignation applies to those circumstances that we are helpless to change, but which we must trust are in harmony with the most comprehensive Divine Justice, even if we cannot perceive it. On the other hand, we are commanded to work equitably for justice, though never from a sense of personal vindictiveness. Justice is for all of humanity and Mercy has the final word.

ᶜAdhāb: عذاب Chastisement, punishment, torment.

The essential meaning of this word is the kind of punishment that serves as a warning to others and prevents the offender from continuing the offense. It is not merely arbitrary torment nor vindictive retribution. This might lead one to reflect that being veiled form God's signs is its own punishment and brings with it inevitable consequences. *God has placed a seal on their heart and hearing, and their vision is veiled. Their punishment is great.* (Sūrah al-Baqarah 2:7)

Ahl: أهل The People. According to Muḥammad Asad: The term *ahl* denotes primarily the "people" of one town, country, or family, as well as the "fellow-members" of one race, religion, profession, etc. In its wider, ideological sense it is applied to people who have certain characteristics in common, e.g., *ahl al-ᶜilm* ("people of knowledge," i.e., scholars), or who follow one and the same persuasion or belief, e.g., *ahl al-kitāb* ("the followers of [earlier] revelation"), *ahl al-Qur'ān* ("the followers of the Qur'ān"), and so forth. (Asad, *Sūrah ash-Shūrā* 42:45, note 46)

Ahl aṣ-Ṣūffa: أهل الصفة The people of the bench. These were companions of the Prophet who lived in voluntary poverty in the *Masjid* (mosque) in order to devote themselves to spiritual development. They are thought to be an inner circle who received spiritual teachings from Muḥammad.

Aḥmad: أحمد The Celestial Name of Muḥammad, meaning "the Most Praiseworthy of those who praise Allāh."

Al-Akhfā: الأخفى The innermost consciousness. A term from Islamic metaphysics which literally means "the most secret." It is said to be the inner human reality that is experienced by those who purify their consciousness and penetrate to the core of their being where they are closest to God.

Al-Ākhirah: الآخرة The Hereafter, Eternity. The afterlife is what the soul will experience after death, and what we should keep in mind during this life. It is the state where we will experience certain things mentioned in the Qur'ān: the Bridge, the Scales, the Garden, and the Fire. The spiritual development of the soul will determine the conditions and quality of our experience of the Hereafter.

For the traveler on the spiritual path these realities may be experienced, to some extent, even here in this life. It is the state of inner expansiveness that we can know in this life by emptying ourselves of worldly and egoistic concerns and preoccupations. The *Ākhirah* will be experienced to the extent that we are virtuous, freed from the limitations of our physical existence, and able to live in the state of remembrance, *dhikr Allāh*.

Akhlāq: أخلاق Positive traits of character, especially those noble and beautiful qualities that were perfected and modeled by the Prophet Muḥammad ﷺ. See also: ***Khuluq***.

Alast, Covenant of: عهد ألست While human beings were subsisting within God prior to creation, God asked them "Am I not (*alast*) your Lord?" And they all answered "Yes! We testify!" At the Resurrection it will be determined whether each individual remained faithful to his original testimony. In other words, did his actions reflect his pre-creation acceptance of servanthood and God's Lordship? Or did his actions demonstrate that he lived the life of a denier, one whose life was a denial of the Covenant of *Alast*?

ᶜAlaq: علق An infinitesimal, clinging substance; a germ cell. This word is used in the first *āyāts* revealed to Muḥammad: *Read, in the name of your Sustainer who created, created the human being from ᶜalaq* (*Sūrah al-ᶜAlaq* 96:1-2). Unfortunately, too often it has been translated in a very unscientific way as "blood clot," an objectionable translation, for anyone acquainted with a minimum of biological science. If we look into the Arabic word, however, we see that *ᶜalaqa* means establishing some sort of relationship, and *ᶜalaq* also describes anything that has a linking capacity. In the age of bio-engineering are we really going to maintain a translation of "clot" for *ᶜalaq*, or can we find something general enough and yet able to convey some of the scientific accuracy that is actually implied by the term? *ᶜAlaq* could, for instance, be descriptive of DNA's double helix. It need not, however, be translated by something as specific as DNA, because as science develops, this understanding may be surpassed. The challenge is to find a translation that better embodies the essential meaning and that does not mislead us into unproductive areas of thought.

Allāh: الله The Divinity; the God of all religions, who is beyond any description or limitation. All of manifest existence reflects the qualities and will of Allāh. Allāh is the essential Truth (*Al-Ḥaqq*) of existence. The Qurʾān, which refers to itself as "guidance for humanity" (*Sūrah al-Baqarah* 2:185), speaks so often and in so many contexts about God, and all of these contexts must be interiorized into a wholeness in order to do justice to the comprehensive notion of Allāh. The word "Allāh" is used 2,697 times in the Qurʾān.

The Qurʾān works by drawing our attention to certain evident facts—primarily the beauty, order, and intelligence evidenced in human nature and the natural world—and turning these facts into "reminders" of the existence of a benevolent intelligent Being.

In the Qur'ān, *Sūrah al-Ikhlāṣ* offers us the most concise indication of the essential attributes of the Divine.

> *SAY: "He is the One God:*
> *God the Eternal, the Uncaused Cause of All That Exists (aṣ-Ṣamad).*
> *He begets not, and neither is He begotten;*
> *and there is nothing that could be compared with Him." (Sūrah al-Ikhlāṣ* 112:1-4*)*

Muḥammad Asad comments as follows: This rendering gives no more than an approximate meaning of the term *aṣ-Ṣamad,* which occurs in the Qur'ān only once, and is applied to God alone. It comprises the concepts of Primary Cause and eternal, independent Being, combined with the idea that everything existing or conceivable goes back to Him as its source and is, therefore, dependent on Him for its beginning as well as for its continued existence."

The fact that God is One and unique in every respect, without beginning and without end, has its logical correlate in the statement that *there is nothing that could be compared with Him*—thus precluding any possibility of describing or defining Him. Consequently, the *quality* of His Being is beyond the range of human comprehension or imagination: which also explains why any attempt at "depicting" God by means of figurative representations or even abstract symbols must be qualified as a blasphemous denial of the truth.

ᶜAmal: عمل Work or action. Spiritual development is a kind of Work. When knowledge combines with action, true well-being is attained. According to the words of the Prophet ﷺ: "He who acts upon what he knows, Allāh will make him inherit that which he does not know."

This word also has the deeper sense that what we do with intention, sincerity, and a sense of meaning is true "action." In other words, *ᶜamal,* true action, is not just "going through the motions," it is something from deep within us. The Qurʾān reminds us continually that there is a connection between keeping faith (*amānu*) and righteous action (*ʿamilu*): *wa ʾāmanu wa ʿamul uṣ-ṣāliḥāt.*

Amānah: أمانة Trust. This is the ultimate trust or covenant between Allāh and the human being. *Verily, We did offer the trust [of reason and volition] to the heavens, and the earth, and the mountains: but they refused to bear it because they were afraid of it. Yet man took it up; for, verily, he has always been prone to be most wicked, most foolish.* (*Sūrah al-Aḥzāb* 33:72) (It would seem that Allāh is not without a certain wry sense of humor here. And yet the honor and burden of responsibility continues to rest with this foolish humanity. ~Kabir Helminski)

Asad continues: The classical commentators give all kinds of laborious explanations to the term *amānah* ("trust") occurring in this parable, but the most convincing of them are "reason," or "intellect," and "the faculty of volition"—i.e., the ability to choose between two or more possible courses of action or modes of behavior, and thus between good and evil." (Asad, *Sūrah al-Aḥzāb* 33:72, note 87)

Behold, God bids you to deliver all that you have been entrusted with unto those who are entitled thereto, and whenever you judge between people, to judge with justice. Verily, most excellent is what God exhorts you to do: verily, God is all-hearing, all-seeing! (*Sūrah an-Nisāʿ* 4:58) "To judge with justice" [is] in the judicial sense, as well as in the sense of judging other people's motives, attitudes and behavior. The term *amānah* denotes anything one has been entrusted with, be it in the physical or moral sense (Rāzī). If one reads this ordinance in the context of the verses that precede and follow it, it becomes obvious that it relates to the message or—in view of the plural form *amānāt*—to the truths which have been conveyed to the believers by means of the divine writ, and which they must regard as a sacred trust, to be passed on to "those who are entitled thereto"—i.e., to all mankind, for whom the message of the Qurʾān has been intended. This, of course, does not preclude the ordinance from having a wider scope as well—that is, from its being applied to any material object or moral responsibility which may have been entrusted to a believer—and, in particular, to the exercise of worldly power and political sovereignty by the Muslim community or a Muslim state (to which the next verse, 4:59 refers). (Asad, *Sūrah an-Nisā*ᶜ 4:58, note 75)

Amr: أمر Guidance, directive, indication. *Al-amāratu wat-tʾamūr* means a sign post made of small stones in the desert to indicate either the boundaries or to show the direction. *They will ask you about the Spirit; say to them: the Spirit proceeds from the Directive (al-Amr) of my Rabb.* (*Sūrah al-Isrā*ᶜ 17:85)

Arabic has two words to indicate the Divine creative process. Amr is God's directive energy even before it manifests in physical form. Its creation or manifestation in the physical world is described by the word "khalq."

The laws that determine how things will manifest in the universe are from the world of Divine Planning (*ᶜĀlam ul-Amr*), but they are expressed and realized in the world of creation (*ᶜĀlam ul-Khalq*).

ᶜAql: عقل Intellect; reason, understanding. It is the principle of reason that distinguishs us from animals, for although animals are not completely devoid of it, it is in the human being that reason can govern other faculties such as instinct, desire, and emotion. However, *ᶜAql* or Intellect has many degrees: Ibn Rushd (Averroes, d. 595/1198), the chief interpreter of Aristotle, expressed the idea that *ᶜAql* operated at all metaphysical levels, from the Cosmos (the grand totality of all spiritual levels) to the Macrocosm (all of material existence) to the Microcosm (the human being). True Intellect, however, can be veiled or obscured by that kind of compulsive intellectuality that is mere thinking devoid of the cognitive power of the Heart.

From Asad's commentary: *Give, then, this glad tiding to My servants who listen to all that is said, and follow the best of it: for it is they whom God has graced with His guidance, and it is they who are endowed with insight!* (*Sūrah az-Zumar* 39:17-18) According to Rāzī, this describes people who examine every religious proposition (in the widest sense of this term) in the light of their own reason, accepting that which their reason finds to be valid or possible, and rejecting all that does not measure up to the test of reason. In Rāzī's words, the above verse expresses "a praise and commendation following the evidence supplied by one's reason (*ḥujjat al-ᶜaql*), and of reaching one's conclusions in accordance with [the results of] critical examination (*naẓar*) and logical inference (*istidlāl*)." (Asad, *Sūrah az-Zumar* 39:18, note 22) See also: **Taffakur.**

Al-ᶜĀrif: العارف The knower (of Allāh). The one who has been granted Divine Knowledge, *maᶜrifah,* which is a light that Allāh casts into the hearts of whomever He will. This knowing includes truly knowing oneself according to the *Ḥadīth Qudsī*: "Whoever knows himself, knows his *Rabb* (Sustainer)."

ᶜArsh: عرش Throne (of God). *And you will see the angels surrounding the throne of [God's] Almightiness, extolling their Sustainer's glory and praise* (*Sūrah az-Zumar* 39:75). Whenever the term *al-ᶜarsh* ("the throne [of God]") occurs in the Qur'ān, it is used as a metaphor for His absolute dominion over all that exists. The term *ᶜarsh* (lit., "throne" or, more properly, "seat of power") denotes God's absolute sway over all that exists; hence, the expression *dhu'l-ᶜarsh* may be suitably rendered as "He who is enthroned in His almightiness." Since God is infinite in space as well as in time, it is obvious that His "throne" (*ᶜarsh*) has a purely metaphorical connotation, circumscribing His absolute, unfathomable sway over all that exists or possibly could exist. All Muslim commentators, classical and modern, are unanimously of the opinion that the use of *ᶜarsh* in the Qur'ān is metaphorical and is meant to express God's absolute sway over all His creation. It is noteworthy that in all the seven instances where God is spoken of in the Qur'ān as "established on the throne of His almightiness" (7:54, 10:3, 13:2, 20:5, 25:59, 32:4, and 57:4) this expression is connected with a declaration of His having created the universe. (Asad, *Sūrah az-Zumar* 39:75, note 77; *Sūrah al-Isrāᶜ* 17:42, note 50; *Sūrah al-Aᶜrāf* 7:54 note 43)

They who bear [within themselves the knowledge of] the throne of [God's] almightiness, as well as all who are near it, extol their Sustainer's limitless glory and praise, and have faith in Him, and ask forgiveness for all [others] who have attained to faith (*Sūrah Ghāfir* 40:7). "All who are near it" is literally "around it": cf., Zamakhsharī's explanation of the expression *ḥawlahā* occurring in 27:8 in the sense of "near it." In his commentary on 40:7, Bayḍāwī states explicitly that the "bearing" of God's throne of almightiness (*al-ᶜarsh*) must be understood in a metaphorical sense: "Their carrying it and surrounding it [or "being near it"] is a metaphor of their being mindful of it and acting in accordance therewith, or a metonym for their closeness to the Lord of the Throne, their dignity in His sight, and their being instrumental in the realization of His will." The rendering of the above verse reflects Bayḍāwī's interpretation. As regards the beings which are said to be close to the throne of God's almightiness, most of the classical commentators—obviously basing their view on the symbolic image of "the angels surrounding the throne of [God's] almightiness" on the Day of Judgment (39:75)—think in this instance, too, exclusively of angels. But whereas it cannot be denied that the present verse refers *also* to angels, it does not follow that it refers *exclusively* to them. In its abstract connotation, the verb *ḥamala* frequently signifies "he bore [or "took upon himself"] the *responsibility* [for something]": and so it is evident that it applies here not only to angels but also to all human beings who are conscious of the tremendous implications of the concept of God's almightiness and hence feel morally responsible for translating this consciousness into the reality of their own and their fellow-beings' lives. (Asad, *Sūrah Ghāfir* 40:7, note 4)

Al Asmāᶜul-Ḥusnā: الأسماء الحسنة Attributes, the Most Beautiful Names; *ṣifāt*. *And God's [alone] are the attributes of perfection: invoke Him, then, by these, and stand aloof from all who distort the meaning of His attributes: they shall be requited for all that they were wont to do!*" (*Sūrah al-Aᶜrāf* 7:180) This passage connects with the mention, at the end of the preceding verse, of "the heedless ones" who do not use their faculty of discernment in the way intended for it by God, and remain heedless of Him who comprises within Himself all the attributes of perfection and represents, therefore, the Ultimate Reality. As regards the expression *al-asmāʾ al-ḥusnā* (lit., "the most perfect [or "most goodly"] names"), which occurs in the Qurʾān four times—i.e., in the above verse as well as in 17:110, 20:8, and 59:24—it is to be borne in mind that the term *ism* (name) is, primarily, a word applied to denote the substance or the intrinsic attributes of an object under consideration, while the term *al-ḥusnā* is the plural form of *al-aḥsan* ("that which is best" or "most goodly"). Thus, the combination of *al-asmāʾ al-ḥusnā* may be appropriately rendered as "the attributes of perfection"—a term reserved in the Qur'ān for God alone.

Limitless is He in His glory, and sublimely exalted above anything that men may devise by way of definition (*Sūrah al-An*ʿ*ām* 6:100). Utterly remote is He from all imperfection and from the incompleteness which is implied in the concept of having progeny. The very concept of "definition" implies the possibility of a comparison or correlation of an object with other objects; God, however, is unique, there being *nothing like unto Him* (42:11) and therefore, *nothing that could be compared with Him* (112:4)—with the result that any attempt at defining Him or His "attributes" is a logical impossibility and, from the ethical point of view, a sin. The fact that He is undefinable makes it clear that the "attributes" (*ṣifāt*) of God mentioned in the Qur'ān do not circumscribe His reality but, rather, the perceptible *effect of His activity* on and within the universe created by Him. (Asad, *Sūrah al-A*ʿ*rāf* 7:180 note 145; *Sūrah al-An*ʿ*ām* 6:100 note 88)

Āyah: آية Sign, Symbol, Message, Verse. According to Muḥammad Asad: *Truly did he [the Prophet] see some of the most profound of his Sustainer's symbols* (*āyāt*, pl. of *āyah*) (*Sūrah an-Najm* 53:18). The term *āyāt* is used in *Sūrah al-Isrā*ʿ 17:1 in reference to the same mystic experience, namely, the Ascension. *Limitless in His glory is He who transported His servant by night from the Inviolable House of Worship [at Mecca] to the Remote House of Worship [at Jerusalem]—the environs of which We had blessed—so that We might show him some of Our symbols: for, verily, He alone is all-hearing, all-seeing.* Although the term *āyah* is most frequently used in the Qur'ān in the sense of "[divine] message," we must remember that, primarily, it denotes "a sign [or "token"] by which a thing is known" (*Qāmūs*). As defined by Rāghib, it signifies any perceivable phenomenon (irrespective of whether it is apparent to the senses or only to the intellect) connected with a thing that is not, by itself, similarly perceivable: in brief, a "symbol."

When Gabriel tells Mary she will conceive Jesus, she is told: *So that We might make him a symbol unto mankind and an act of grace from Us* (*Sūrah Maryam* 19:21). One of the several meanings of the term *āyah* is "a sign," or, as elaborately defined by Rāghib, "a symbol." However the sense in which *āyah* is most frequently used in the Qur'ān is "a [divine] message": hence, its metonymic application to Jesus may mean that he was destined to become a vehicle of God's message to man—i.e., a prophet—and, thus, a symbol of God's grace. *No message of their Sustainer's messages ever reaches them without their turning away from it* (*Sūrah Yā Sīn* 36:46) or *no sign of their Sustainer's signs* since the noun *āyah* denotes "a message" as well as "a sign." The word *āyah* is also used to denote a "verse" of the Qurʾān because every one of these verses contains a message.

Miracles are in the power of God alone (*Sūrah al-Anʿām* 6:109). It is to be noted that the Qurʾānic term *āyah* denotes not only a "miracle" (in the sense of a happening that goes beyond the usual—that is, commonly observable—course of nature), but also a "sign" or "message": and the last-mentioned significance is the one which is by far the most frequently met with in the Qurʾān. Thus, what is commonly described as a "miracle" constitutes, in fact, an *unusual message* from God, indicating—sometimes in a symbolic manner—a spiritual truth which would otherwise have remained hidden from man's intellect. But even such extraordinary, "miraculous" messages cannot be regarded as "supernatural": for the so-called "laws of nature" are only a perceptible manifestation of "God's way" (*sunnat Allāh*) in respect of His creation—and, consequently, everything that exists and happens, or could conceivably exist or happen, is "natural" in the innermost sense of this word, irrespective of whether it conforms to the ordinary course of events or goes beyond it. Now since the extraordinary messages referred to manifest themselves, as a rule, through the instrumentality of those specially gifted and elected personalities known as "prophets," these are sometimes spoken of as "performing miracles"—a misconception which the Qurʾān removes by the words, *Miracles are in the power of God alone.* (Asad, *Sūrah an-Najm* 53:18 note 12; *Sūrah al-Isrāʿ* 17:1 note 2; *Sūrah Maryam* 19:21 note 16; *Sūrah Yā Sīn* 36:46 note 25; *Sūrah al-Baqarah* 2:106 note 87; *Sūrah al-Anʿām* 6:109 note 94)

Awliyāʿ: أولياء The friends of Allāh; the saints. They are those who have been made pure by Allāh and who are able to sustain remembrance of Him. The *awliyāʿ* are honored because they contain and reflect the attributes of Allāh.

ʿAyn al-Yaqīn: عين اليقين The eye of certainty, which is equivalent to the eye of the heart. This is the second of three stages of knowledge or "certainty." The first is *ᶜilm al-yaqīn*, the knowledge of certainty, which is knowing from being told about something. *ᶜAyn al-yaqīn* is the certainty that comes from actually seeing or experiencing something. *Ḥaqq al-yaqīn* is the certainty that comes from a deep familiarity with something.

Baqāᶜ: بقاء Subsistence, the realization that your existence is supported by the Divine. This term is associated with its complement, *fanāᶜ*, which means annihilation of the self in the Being of Allāh. This is the experience of certain mystics who experience the dissolving of the self into the Divine Presence, which is said to be followed by the experience of "subsistence."

All that dwells upon the earth is perishing, yet there subsists the Face of your Sustainer, Majestic, Splendid (*Sūrah ar-Raḥmān* 55:26-27). Al-Ghazālī wrote: "Each thing has two faces, a face of its own, and a face of its Lord; in respect to its own face it is nothingness, and in respect to the Face of God it is Being. Thus there is nothing in existence save only God and His Face, for everything is perishing except His Face." See ***Fanāᶜ***.

Barakah: بركة Effective grace; spiritual energy. When it is said that a person has *barakah* it suggests the ability of putting into action the divine attributes of supra-conscious mind.

Barakah is spiritual influence, blessing, or grace. Certain persons, places, and things can be the vehicle for *baraka*, while others may dispel it. It comes from the root meaning "to settle," implying the Divine influence that God sends down. It is found in many greetings such as *bāraka 'llāhu fīk* ("May God bless you").

Barzakh: برزخ Interworld, lit. isthmus. In Islamic metaphysics this is an intermediate visionary realm between material existence and pure meaning; *mundus imaginalis*. The *Barzakh* is the locus of imaginal experience. It is here that the spiritually-developed soul receives inspiration, guidance, and wisdom in the form of dreams and visions. The *Barzakh* is also what contains the soul in the afterlife: *There is a barzakh (barrier) until the Day when all will be raised from the dead* (*Sūrah al-Muᶜminūn* 23:100).

Baṣīrah: بصيرة Seeing, insight. According to Asad: Derived from the verb *baṣura* or *baṣira* ("he became seeing" or "he saw"), the noun *baṣīrah* (as also the verb) has the abstract connotation of "seeing with one's mind" and so it signifies "the faculty of understanding based on conscious insight" as well as "an evidence accessible to the intellect" or "verifiable by the intellect." (Asad, *Sūrah Yūsuf* 12:108 note 104; see also ***Taffakur***)

I have gained insight into something which they were unable to see (*Sūrah Ṭā Hā* 20:96). It is to be noted that the verb *baṣura* (lit., "he became seeing") has the tropical significance of "he perceived [something] mentally," or "he gained insight," or "he understood." (Asad, *Sūrah Ṭā Hā* 20:96 note 81)

Now had it been Our will [that men should not be able to discern between right and wrong], We could surely have deprived them of their sight, so that they would stray forever from the right way: for how could they have had insight? (*Sūrah Yā Sīn* 36:66) The verb *baṣura* ("he became seeing" or "he saw") is obviously used in its tropical sense of "perceiving [something] mentally." According to Ibn 'Abbās, as quoted by Ṭabarī, the phrase *annā yubṣirūn* signifies "how could they perceive the truth?" (Asad, *Sūrah Yā Sīn* 36:66 note 34)

They perished because Satan had made their sinful doings seem goodly to them and thus had barred them from the path of God despite their having been endowed with the ability to perceive the truth (*Sūrah al-ᶜAnkabūt* 29:38). Thus, the Qurʾān implies that it is man's "ability to perceive the truth" (*istibṣār*) that makes him morally responsible for his doings and, hence, for his failure to resist his own evil impulses—which is evidently the meaning of "Satan" in this context.

The Eye of the Heart can discern values and receive spiritual knowledge. True Seeing is an attribute of God that is shared with the spiritualized human being. *Say, This is my path. I call to God on clear evidence and by insight, I and whoever follows me.* (*Sūrah Yūsuf* 12:108).

The above *āyāh*, often used as a pledge of loyalty (*bayᶜat*), points to the degree of insight that was given to Muḥammad, and that is available to those of his community who follow him.

"Fear the discernment (*firāsa*) of the believer (*muᶜmin*), for he sees with the light of God."[25]

Al-Bāṭin: الباطن The Inner (*Sūrah al-Ḥadīd* 57:3); one of God's names. *Bāṭin* can also mean what is hidden, esoteric, or initiatory. See also: ***Ẓāhir***, the Manifest.

Bayān: بيان Articulate Thought and Speech. *The Most Gracious has imparted this Qur'ān [unto man]. He has created man: He has imparted unto him articulate thought and speech* (*Sūrah ar-Raḥmān* 55:1-4). The term *al-bayān*—denoting "the means whereby a thing is [intellectually] circumscribed and made clear" (Rāghib)—applies to both thought and speech inasmuch as it comprises the faculty of making a thing or an idea apparent to the mind and conceptually distinct from other things or ideas, as well as the power to express this cognition clearly in spoken or written language (*Tāj al-'Arūs*): hence, in the above context, "articulate thought and speech," recalling the "knowledge of all the names" (i.e., the faculty of conceptual thinking) with which man is endowed (see 2:31…). (Asad, *Sūrah ar-Raḥmān* 55:4 note 1)

Bidᶜah: بدعة Unjustified innovation in matters related to the *sharīᶜah*, the sacred law. For some Muslims, this term has come to mean the insidious innovation of ideas or religious practices that did not exist during the lifetime of the Prophet. *Bidᶜah*, in this sense, is considered a major sin. However, given the changing circumstances of human life, most exponents of Islamic law acknowledge the possibility of positive innovation, *bidᶜah ḥasanah*, bearing in mind that such an innovation would be in harmony with an essential Islamic spirit. An example of such an innovation might be the use of electrical power in amplifying the *adhān*, the call to prayer. It is important to note that nowhere in the Qur'ān, itself, is the term *bidᶜah* used to signify a sin.

Ḍalāl: ضلال Going astray. *[This, then, is] the parable of those who are bent on denying their Sustainer: all their works are as ashes which the wind blows about fiercely on a stormy day: they cannot achieve any benefit whatever from all*

[25] At-Tirmidhī, "Tafsīr al-Qur'ān," 6.

[the good] that they may have wrought: for this [denial of God] is indeed the farthest one can go astray (*Sūrah Ibrāhīm* 14:18). According to Muḥammad Asad: Literally, "this, this is the straying far away." The definite article in the expression *aḍ-ḍalāl al-baʿīd*, preceded by the pronouns *dhālika huwa*, is meant to stress the extreme degree of this "straying far away" or "going astray": a construction that can be rendered in English only by a paraphrase such as that used in this translation. It is to be noted that this phrase occurs in the Qurʾān only twice, in this passage and 22:12, and refers in both cases to a denial, conscious or implied, of God's oneness and uniqueness.

They who will not believe in the life to come are [bound to lose themselves] in suffering and in a profound aberration (*Sūrah Sabāʿ* 34:8). *Ḍalāl,* literally "error" or "going astray," can be translated here as "remote aberration." The construction of this phrase points definitely to suffering in *this* world (in contrast with the suffering in the hereafter spoken of in 34:5 *whereas for those who strive against Our messages, seeking to defeat their purpose, there is grievous suffering in store as an outcome of [their] vileness.* (The particle *min* (lit., "out of") which precedes the noun *rijz,* "vileness" or "vile conduct," indicates that the suffering which awaits such sinners in the life to come is an organic *consequence* of their deliberately evil conduct in this world.) For whereas the concept of "aberration" is meaningless in the context of the life to come, it has an obvious meaning in the context of the moral and social confusion—and, hence, of the individual and social suffering—which is the unavoidable consequence of people's loss of belief in the existence of absolute moral values and, thus, in an ultimate divine judgment on the basis of those values.

[But the keepers of hell] will ask, "Is it not [true] that your apostles came unto you with all evidence of the truth?" Those [in the fire] will say, "Yea, indeed." [And the keepers of hell] will say, "Pray, then!"—for the prayers of those who deny the truth cannot lead to aught but delusion. (*Sūrah Ghāfir* 40:50) According to the classical commentators, the answer "Pray, then!" implies no more than a refusal on the part of the "keepers of hell" to intercede for the doomed sinners, telling them, as it were, "Pray yourselves, if you can." It seems to me, however, that we have here an indirect allusion to the sinners' erstwhile, blasphemous devotion to false objects of worship and false values—the meaning being, "Pray now to those imaginary

powers to which you were wont to ascribe a share in God's divinity, and see whether they can help you!" This interpretation finds support in the next sentence, which speaks of the delusion (*ḍalāl*) inherent in the prayers of "those who deny the truth," i.e., during their life on earth—for, obviously, on the Day of Judgment all such delusions will have disappeared. (Asad, *Sūrah Ibrāhīm* 14:18 note 25; *Sūrah Sabāʿ* 34:8 note 5; *Sūrah Ghāfir* 40:50 note 34)

Dhāt: ذات Essence. This technical metaphysical term was derived from the feminine form of *dhū*, which means "in possession of." Thus it signifies what something essentially is, distinguished from its attributes, *ṣifāt*. It corresponds to the Greek *ousia*, and Latin *essentia*. The *Dhāt*, or Essence of Allāh is what God is apart from His creation, which we are warned not to speculate about since it is inconceivable by the human mind.

While the word *Hu*, a masculine pronoun, refers to God's unmanifest being, here a feminine noun expresses the same unmanifest essence. Ultimately the Divine is beyond any attributes of gender.

Dhawq: ذوق Taste, direct experience of truth. Jeremy Henzell-Thomas writes: *Dhawq* is similar to the words "sapience," or wisdom, derived from the Latin *sapere*, which means primarily to taste and by extension, to "discriminate," "to know." As the Sufi dictum goes: "He who tastes, knows." "Ultimately, real knowledge of [the food and life of the soul] is the 'tasting of its flavour,' the 'spiritual savouring' (*dhawq*) that men of discernment speak of, which almost simultaneously unveils the reality and truth of the matter to the spiritual vision (*kashf*)."[26]

Dhikr: ذكر Remembrance. The invocation of the Divine Name. The state of awareness of the Divine Presence.

The word refers both to memory and to speech. Its literal interpretation is "mention." Hence when the Qurʾān is translated into English,

[26] Syed Muḥammad Naguib Al-Attas, *The Concept of Education in Islām: A Framework for an Islamic Philosophy of Education*. Kuala Lumpur: International Institute of Islamic Thought and Civilisation (ISTAC), 1980, pp. 24-25.

passages that refer to "remembering Allāh" could just as well be translated as "invoking Allāh."

Remember God as He has guided you (*Sūrah al-Baqarah* 2:98). This deceptively simple statement enjoins us to remember and suggests that we have been "guided" to this remembrance by "God." Remembrance is a translation of the Arabic word *dhikr* which has a number of meanings including "mentioning" and "remembering." "Remember" is a word that can be traced back to Middle English and Old French and comes from the Latin *rememorare*. To remember, however, is not simply the calling up of something from the past, but a calling to mind, a state of retaining something in one's awareness. We are reminded to remember by the one who instilled remembrance in us.

This remembrance has an essential nature beyond forms, which can be practiced anywhere and any time. *And remembrance is the greatest. And God knows all that you do* (*Sūrah al-ᶜAnkabūt* 29:45).

At the same time it has its specific forms, or exercises, which lead to experiences on different levels within our own being. Al-Ghazzālī, one of the greatest formulators and interpreters of Islamic spirituality, gave these instructions regarding the practice of remembrance:

> Let your heart be in such a state that the existence or non-existence of anything is the same—that is, let there be no dichotomy of positive and negative. Then sit alone in a quiet place, free of any task or preoccupation, be it the reciting of the Quran, thinking about its meaning, concern over the dictates of religion, or what you have read in books—let nothing beside God enter the mind. Once you are seated in this manner, start to pronounce with your tongue, "Allāh, Allāh," keeping your thought on it.
>
> Practice this continuously and without interruption; you will reach a point when the motion of the tongue will cease, and it will appear as if the word just flows from it spontaneously. You go on in this way until every trace of the tongue movement disappears while the heart registers the thought or idea of the word.
>
> Continuing with the invocation, there will come a time when the word will leave the heart completely. Only the palpable essence or reality of the name will remain, binding itself ineluctably to the heart.
>
> Up to this point everything will have been dependent on your own conscious will; the Divine bliss and enlightenment that may follow have

nothing to do with your conscious will or choice. What you have done so far is to open the window, as it were. You have laid yourself exposed to what God may breathe upon you, as He has done upon His prophets and saints.

If you follow what is said above, you can be sure that the light of Truth will dawn upon your heart. At first intermittently, like flashes of lightning, it will come and go. Sometimes when it comes back it may stay longer than other times. Sometimes it may stay only briefly.

The method of attaining the Truth begins with this simple and beautiful practice of repeating "Allāh," the essential name of God. Just by moving the tongue with a certain intention and presence of mind we are taken into the reality of the Name until "only the palpable essence or reality of the name will remain, binding itself ineluctably to the heart." Through this simple process, the "remembrance" is transferred from the tongue to the mind, from the mind to the feelings and the deeper levels of the self, until its reality is established in the core of the human being.

More and more, remembrance begins to fill one's life. Instead of the usual inner dialogs, commentaries, judgments, and opinions that make up the majority of people's inner life, we may begin to experience the breath and rhythm of remembrance. The divine names are seen to be alive, animate, spiritually prolific—much more real than the repetitive scripts of our superficial personality.

This practice requires no exceptional leap of faith, no abandonment of reason, no complex theology or intellectual attainment. The simple, mindful invocation of God's essential name will take us to the reality of what is being remembered.

The remembrance that begins with the tongue can guide us to the remembrance of the Heart. Perhaps it is evidence of the divine generosity that what begins with the simple repetition of a word could lead to the Secret of secrets. The repetition of the word "Allāh" focuses our thought on God. The rhythm of remembrance inevitably affects brainwaves, and the superficial layers of the mind are calmed. In this transparent stillness of the superficial mind, a deeper level of mind becomes revealed. It is that deeper level of mind, called heart, which is capable of perceiving "something" that is neither apparent to the intellect nor to the senses. It seems as if becoming aware of this "something" has the effect of clarifying the mind, harmonizing the emotions, enhancing the senses, and bringing peace (stillness, rest) to the heart. *Indeed in the remembrance of God hearts find rest* (*Sūrah al-Muᶜminūn* 23:28).

> *And contain yourself patiently at the side of all who invoke their Sustainer, mornings and evenings, seeking His face, nor allow your eyes to go beyond them in search of the attractions of this world's life, and pay no attention to any whose heart We have made unaware of all remembrance of Us because he had always followed his own desires, abandoning all that is just and true. (Sūrah al-Kahf* 18:28*)*

Westerners who are familiar with various spiritual paths may ask, "What is the difference between *dhikr* and meditation?" If by meditation is meant that refined "listening within," the activation of a presence capable of witnessing inner and outer events without becoming absorbed in them, then there is much in common. We can, however, distinguish *dhikr* from the more superficial "technique of concentration"—that is, meditation understood as an exercise performed by an individual for individual purposes such as attaining calmness, clarity, or relaxation. While *dhikr* must include that state of concentration, it is more than that. Remembrance of God is presence realized in relationship with that infinite Being which is both nearer to us than ourselves and, at the same time, greater than anything we can conceive. It is also experienced as loving and being loved by Love.

While the invocation of the names or attributes of God is a primary practice, this remembrance can and should permeate all the range of human capacities and activities.

Remembrance also consists in the mental and emotional recognition that everything is a manifestation of a single Source. Allāh is the Oneness, and all of manifest existence reflects the qualities and will of Allāh, the life and being of Allāh. As we see the budding of flowers in spring we recognize *Al-Khāliq*, the Creator, or *Al-Laṭīf*, the Subtle, and *Al-Muṣawwir*, the Bestower of Form. When we see the power of a great storm or an earthquake, we recognize and remember *Al-ᶜAzīz*, the Mighty, and *Al-Jabbār*, the Compeller. When we view the incredible balance within the ecology of nature we may recognize *Ar-Razzāq*, the Provider; *Al-Wahhāb*, the

Bestower; *Al-Muḥyī*, the Giver of Life; and *Aṣ-Ṣabūr*, the Patient.

As we deepen in recognizing the Attributes we may be led more and more to a sense of awe, and to spontaneous appreciation, thankfulness for the invisible order that manifests existence. As it is said in the Qur^ʾān, *Wheresoever you turn is the Face of God* (*Sūrah al-Baqarah* 2:115). The one who remembers God acquires a sensitivity to the manifest world as well as a sense of the numinous dimensions of existence. More and more the traditional religious terminology of "praise" and "glorification" may correspond to what we are experiencing. We may be led to experiences of such power and beauty that our everyday remembrance may be colored by the memory of these events as well. We may wish to remember the intensity of those experiences in which the veils between the earthly and the divine became very thin.

And thus have We bestowed from on high this [divine writ] as a discourse in the Arabic tongue, and have given therein many facets to all manner of warnings, so that men might remain conscious of Us, or that it give rise to a new awareness in them (*Sūrah Ṭā Hā* 20:113). According to Asad this literally means: "so that they might be or remain God-conscious, or that it create for them a remembrance" i.e., of God. The verb *aḥdatha* signifies "he brought something into existence," i.e., newly or for the first time, while the noun *dhikr* denotes "remembrance" as well as the "presence [of something] in the mind" (Rāghib), i.e, awareness. (Asad, *Sūrah Ṭā Hā* 20:113 note 98)

We have now bestowed upon you from on high a divine writ containing all that you ought to bear in mind: will you not, then, use your reason? (*Sūrah al-Anbiyāʿ* 21:10). The term *dhikr*, which primarily denotes a "reminder" or a "remembrance," or, as Rāghib defines it, the "presence [of something] in the mind," has also the meaning of "that *by which* one is remembered," i.e., with praise—in other words, "renown" or "fame"—and, tropically, "honor," "eminence," or "dignity." Hence the above phrase contains, apart from the concept of a "reminder," an indirect allusion to the dignity and happiness to which man may attain by following the spiritual and social precepts laid down in the Qurʾān. By rendering the expression *dhikrukum* as "all that you ought to bear in mind," I have tried to bring out all these meanings. (Asad, *Sūrah al-Anbiyā*ᶜ 21:10, note 13)

*Consider this Qur*ʾ*ān, endowed with all that one ought to remember!* (*Sūrah Ṣād* 38:1). "All that one ought to remember" could alternatively be rendered "endowed with eminence" (Zamakhsharī), since the term *dhikr* (lit., "reminder," or "remembrance") has also the connotation of "that which is remembered," i.e., "renown," "fame," and, tropically, "eminence." The phrase *fīhi dhikrukum* can be translated "wherein is found all that you ought to bear in mind," i.e., in order to attain to dignity and happiness. (Asad, *Sūrah Ṣād* 38:1 note 3)

*And We have indeed made the Qur*ʾ*ān easy to understand and remember: who then is willing to take it to heart?* (*Sūrah al-Qamar* 54:17). The noun *dhikr* primarily denotes "remembrance" or—as defined by Rāghib—the "presence [of something] in the mind." (Asad, *Sūrah al-Qamar* 54:17 note 11)

Dīn: دين Religion. The totality of practices and beliefs concerning ultimate reality. The word *dīn* has a fundamental meaning of an accounting (*dain*, debt). The day of final judgment is called the Day of the *Dīn*, (*Yawm ad-Dīn*), the day when we will find out what our lives *add up to*. Religion in the abstract sense is called *diyānah* and a specific religion is more often called *millah* ("a way").

Here are some of the more important occurrences in the Qurʾān:

Let there be no compulsion in religion (*dīn*). (*Sūrah al-Baqarah* 2:256)

With God the religion is surrender (islām). (*Sūrah Āl* ᶜ*Imrān* 3:19)

Today I have perfected your religion for you. (*Sūrah al-Mā*ᶜ*idah* 5:3)

It is He who has sent His messenger with guidance and religion of Truth, to proclaim it over all religion, even though the idolators (mushrikuun) may detest it. (*Sūrah at-Tawbah* 9:33)

He has chosen you and has laid no difficulties upon you in your religion. (*Sūrah al-Ḥajj* 22:78)

Unto you, your religion, and unto me, mine! (*Sūrah al-Kāfirūn* 109:6)

According to Muḥammad Asad: The term *dīn* denotes both the contents of and the compliance with a morally binding law. Consequently, it signifies "religion" in the widest sense of this term, extending over all that pertains to its doctrinal contents and their practical implications, as well as to man's attitude towards the object of his worship, thus comprising also the concept of "faith." The rendering of *dīn* as "religion," "faith," "religious law," or "moral law" depends on the context in which this term is used.

There shall be no coercion in matters of faith (*dīn*) (*Sūrah al-Baqarah* 2:256). On the strength of the categorical prohibition of coercion (*ikrāh*) in anything that pertains to faith or religion, all Islamic jurists (*fuqahā'*), without any exception, hold that forcible conversion is under all circumstances null and void, and that any attempt at coercing a non-believer to accept the faith of Islām is a grievous sin: a verdict which disposes of the widespread fallacy that Islām places before the unbelievers the alternative of "conversion or the sword." (*Sūrah al-Baqarah* 2:256 note 249)

For more examples of *Dīn* see 42:21, 95:7, 98:5, or 107:1.

Duᶜāᶜ: **دعاء** Supplication (literally, a "call" or "plea"). The spontaneous dialog with Allāh, sometimes expressed in words, sometimes silently in the heart. A *duᶜāᶜ* often is the conclusion of the ritual worship, *ṣalāh,* and is typically performed in silence with hands upraised. *Your Sustainer says, "Call upon Me and I will answer you"* (*Sūrah al-Baqarah* 2:260).

Dunyā: دنيا The world. ***Al-ḥayāt ad-dunyā:*** the present life. The world is not conceived as evil, but when sought as an end in itself it is harmful to our spiritual life. The Qur'ān refers to *those who have purchased the present life at the price of the world to come* (*Sūrah al-Baqarah* 2:86). The *dunyā* has the power to delude us and waylay us from remembrance: *God's promise is true, so don't let the present world delude you* (*Sūrah al-Fāṭir* 35:5). Much of this present life is *nothing but a sport* (*Sūrah al-Anᶜām* 6:32). *To him who desires a harvest in the life to come, We shall grant an increase in his harvest; whereas to him who desires a harvest in this world, We may give something thereof, but he will have no share in the life to come.* (*Sūrah ash-Shūrā* 42:20)

Faqr: **فقر** Spiritual poverty; the condition of realizing that we human beings are "the poor ones" and we depend on Allāh for everything. *O Human beings, you are poor in relation to God, but God is rich and worthy of all praise* (*Sūrah al-Fāṭir* 35:15). This attitude of humility and receptivity was very much a quality of the Prophet Muḥammad ﷺ, who said "Poverty is my pride (*Faqrī fakhrī*)." The essence of spiritual poverty is emptying oneself in order to be receptive to the Divine Presence. This could be compared to the doctrine of *kenosis* in early Christianity.

Fanāᶜ: فناء Annihilation. This is a term used by the mystics to describe the experience of being overwhelmed by the Divine Presence. In such a state one's own individuality seems temporarily to have melted into the Divine Being. Islamically speaking, *fanāʾ* is being overwhelmed by God the way the stars are overwhelmed by the brightness of the sun. This has a number of different meanings, but, practically speaking, it most often means "ego death." The state of *fanāʾ* is followed by or alternates with *baqāᶜ*: the state of one's individuality re-emerging and abiding through the Divine Being.

Fasād: فساد Spreading ruin on this earth. As Islamic Law scholar Khaled Abou El Fadl of UCLA explains in his highly acclaimed new book, *The Great Theft: Wrestling Islam from the Extremists*, these radicals "entirely ignore the Qurʾānic teaching that the act of destroying or spreading ruin on this earth is one of the gravest sins possible—*fasād fil-arḍ*, which means to corrupt the earth by destroying the beauty of creation. This is considered an ultimate act of blasphemy against God. Those who corrupt the earth by destroying lives, property, and nature are designated as *mufsidūn* (corruptors and evildoers) who, in effect, wage war against God by dismantling the very fabric of existence... the crime is called ***Ḥirabāh*** (waging war against society)."

Fayḍ: فيض Grace. The continuous overflowing of the Divine Essence which sustains all of creation. In truth, the grace we receive only depends on our ability to be conscious of and grateful for this overflowing grace.

Fiqh: فقه Jurisprudence. The principles that deal with religious practice and social legislation. Originally this word meant "understanding," and over time it came to be associated with the interpretation and application of the *sharīʿah* (sacred law).

Fitnah: فتنة Rebellion, strife; a test, a trial. *Fitnah* means the oppression that ensues from aggression: *And fight in God's cause against those who wage war against you, but do not commit aggression—for, verily, God does not love aggressors. And slay them wherever you may come upon them, and drive them away from wherever they drove you away—for oppression (fitnah) is even worse than killing.* (*Sūrah al-Baqarah* 2:190-192). Muḥammad Asad writes: "In view of the preceding ordinance, the injunction "slay them wherever you may come upon them" is valid only within the context of hostilities *already in progress* (Rāzī), on the understanding that "those who wage war against you" are the aggressors or oppressors." (*Sūrah al-Baqarah* 2:190-192, note 168)

While *fitnah* has come to mean the strife and oppression that proceeds from sedition or rebellion, its original meaning was a trial or a test. *Your wealth and your children are only a trial.* (*Sūrah at-Taghābun* 64:15)

Fiṭrah: فطرة Our innate nature, or disposition, as it was created by God. The natural disposition to the Good which God has instilled in the human being. *Fiṭrah* is an essential aspect of human nature. There is good in every human being, no matter how much it may be obscured. This innate core may be perverted, distorted, ignored, and denied, but never completely destroyed.

Turn your face toward the essential religion (dīni ḥanīfā), the innate nature (fiṭrah) that was originated (faṭara) by God to be the natural way for people; what God created is not to be substituted. That is authentic religion (dīn ul-qayyim), but most people do not know it. (*Sūrah ar-Rūm* 30:30). This is one of the most intriguing and difficult to translate passages of the Qurʾān.

It is immediately followed by the following two *āyāt*: *And so turn to Him alone, be mindful of Him, establish worship, free from idolizing tendencies, and from those who split up their religion and become sectarian, each exulting in their own faction* (*Sūrah ar-Rūm* 30:31-32).

Furqān: فرقان Discernment. An innate capacity within the human being to make distinctions, especially to discern the good and the true from the bad and the false. *Al-Furqān* is also a synonym for the Holy Qurʾān, which serves as a tool of discernment.

We can come to discern the qualities of the Spirit from the qualities of the compulsive ego. The ego is most concerned with its own survival, comfort, and vanity. The ego is the source of envy, resentment, pride, hypocrisy, guilt, and blame.

Spirit, on the other hand, is inwardly supportive, patient, forgiving, generous with no strings attached, humble without being weak, loving yet impartial.

The individualized Spirit, which we call the soul when it has begun to become aware of itself, can learn to see beyond its immediate identifications in the material and psychological worlds and resonate with Spirit (*Rūḥ*). In this process discernment develops.

Futuwwah: فتوة Islamic Chivalry. The meaning of the word derives from the idea of noble manliness. The ethic of heroic sacrifice and generosity which traces back to the family of the Prophet eventually developed into Orders of *Futuwwah*, which flourished in the Islamic world especially from the eleventh century onwards. As-Sulami wrote an important text, *Kitāb al-Futuwwah* (published as *The Book of Sufi Chivalry*) which explores the values of *Futuwwah*. It is full of noble sentiments such as, "If a brother of yours says, 'Let's go," and you say 'To where?' then you are not a true brother."

Ghaflah: غفلة Heedlessness. This word describes those who "know only the surface appearance of the life of this world, and are heedless of the Hereafter" (30:7). It implies those without *ḥuḍūr*, or presence, and lacking in *taqwā*, mindfulness of God.

Al-Ghafūr: الغفور The Forgiving One who conceals our mistakes.

Al-Ghaffār: الغفار The All-Concealing. The nature of Allāh's forgiveness is that through His generous grace He conceals our faults.

Maghfirah is usually translated as forgiveness but also means protection. *Istighfār* means to desire correction and protection from the consequences of our mistakes and faults.

Al-Ghayb: الغيب The non-manifest; the unseen. The Holy Qur'ān describes itself in *Sūrah al-Baqarah* 2:3 as being: *Guidance for the God-conscious; who keep faith with the Unseen, establish worship, and spend out of what We have provided for them. Al Ghayb* occurs more than 50 times in the Qur'ān pointing repeatedly to a Reality beyond the physical senses. In *Sūrah as-Sajdah* 32:6 it is said, *He is the Knower of the Unseen and the Visible.*

Ḥadīth: حديث A saying of the Prophet ﷺ transmitted outside the Qur'ān through a chain of known intermediaries. There are two kinds of *ḥadīth*: *ḥadīth qudsī* (lit. holy utterance), a direct revelation, in which God speaks in the first person by the mouth of the Prophet, and *ḥadīth nabawī* (prophetic utterance), in which the Prophet speaks as himself.

Al-Ḥajj: الحج The Pilgrimage, one of the five pillars of Islam, is a series of rites enacted in Mecca and its environs at a specific time of year. Because Islam follows a lunar calendar, the time of *Ḥajj* advances about ten days each year. The Pilgrimage is obligatory on those who are healthy enough and financially able to accomplish it without compromising their family responsibilities.

The word *Ḥajj* occurs in the *Qur'ān* ten times and each time the command or direction is for mankind (*an-nās*) and not only for the Muslims or *mu'minūn*; quite unlike *Ṣalāt* or *Zakāt* which are specifically mentioned for Muslims (*Sūrah at-Tawbah* 9:3-22; *Sūrah Āl 'Imrān* 3:97).

The Qur'ān has asked the Muslims to invite all of mankind to come and see what this system is doing for them with their own eyes (*Sūrah al-Ḥajj* 22:28). Moreover, in order to maintain Islam as a universal religion throughout the world, it is necessary to hold international gatherings, basically to demonstrate the universal, egalitarian, and timeless teachings of *Islām*.

Al-Ḥakīm: الحكيم The All-Wise. This Divine Attribute is often found coupled with either *Al-'Aziz*, the "Almighty" (*The bestowal from on high of this divine writ issues from God, the Almighty, the Wise. Sūrah al-Aḥqāf* 46:2) or *Al-ᶜAlīm*, the "All-Knowing" (*thou hast received this Qur'ān out of the grace of One who is Wise, All-Knowing. Sūrah an-Naml* 27:6). But the word *Ḥakīm* also has connotations of "judgment" as in the last *āyah* of *Sūrah at-Tīn: Is not God the wisest of all judges? 'Alaysal-lāhu bi-'Aḥkamīl-ḥākimīn* (*Sūrah at-Tīn* 95:8). See also: **Ḥikmah**: Wisdom.

Ḥalāl, Ḥarām: حلال، حرام Permitted, forbidden. Ḥalāl literally means "released," while Ḥarām means "restricted" or "forbidden." According to Islamic jurisprudence (fiqh), all human actions fall into one of five categories: ḥarām, makrūh (discouraged), mubāḥ (neutral), mustaḥabb (recommended), and farḍ (obligatory).

Hal and Maqām: حال و مقام These terms signify the temporary and more permanent levels of consciousness that are experienced on the journey of spiritual realization. *Hal* signifies a temporary, passing state, while *maqām* is a place of stabilization, a fixed station.

Al-Ḥaqq: الحق The Truth; the Real. This is one of the most frequently used synonyms for Allāh, often being translated simply as God. Its significance, however, is that Allāh is the Most Real. Stemming from the verb *ḥaqqa*, "to be realized, to come true, and to be just," *Al-Ḥaqq* is that which is our purpose on earth to realize or know. *God—He who guides to the Truth* (*Sūrah Yūnus* 10:35).

Ḥaqq also implies what is "right" and the "rights" associated with Justice. The Qur'ān describes the goods left as an inheritance to one's family as "obligations of the God-conscious," *ḥaqqan ᶜalal-mutaqqīn* (*Sūrah al-Baqarah* 2:180).

Finally, it suggests that all of creation exists in accordance with Truth: *It is He who created the heavens and the earth with Truth.* (*Sūrah al-Anᶜām* 6:73). In other words, Truth is inherent in every detail of life; realizing this leads to the realization of Absolute Reality, *Ḥaqīqah*.

Ḥaqīqah: حقيقة The Absolute Reality; the Truth. This metaphysical term is often associated with the sequence: *Sharīᶜah* (The Sacred Law), *Ṭarīqah* (The Spiritual Path), *Maᶜrifah* (Gnosis), *Ḥaqīqah* (The Truth). These represent a development in which the former terms are subsumed into the latter in a progression of spiritual realization. It is like a journey from the circumference of a circle to its center. If the circumference represents the unconscious state of the ego (*nafs*), the radius that leads to the center begins with acceptance of the Sacred Law, the following of the Spirtual Path to the experience of Spiritual Knowledge, until one finally can live in the state of continuous realization of the Truth. *Ḥaqīqah* is also identified with *lubb* ("kernel") as in the Qur᾽ānic phrase: *Can, then, he who knows that whatever has been bestowed from on high upon thee by thy Sustainer is the truth* (*ḥaqqu*) *be deemed equal to one who is blind? Only they who are endowed with insight* (*᾽ulul-᾽albāb*, pl. of *lubb*) *keep this in mind.* (*Sūrah ar-Raᶜd* 13:19).

***Ḥayāᶜ*:** حياء Modesty. "Every religion has its characteristic virtue and that of Islām is modesty." (Hadith) By remembering our servanthood we conceal whatever qualities, strengths, and realizations have been attained by God's grace. Modesty is dignity which does not boast or flaunt itself. Its outward manifestation is modesty in dress.

***Al-Ḥayy*:** الحي The Ever-Living; an attribute of God. It is not merely an expression of biological life, but an eternal attribute that forms the basis of our existence. The spiritual life will be most truly successful when we succeed in bringing life to the heart, through the remembrance of God.

The Holy Qur᾽ān tells us: *O you who have faith! Respond to the call of God and the messenger whenever* ***he calls you to that which will give you life****; and know that God intervenes between man and his desires, and that you shall be gathered back to Him* (*Sūrah al-Anfāl* 8:24). At the beginning of the *āyah* we are told, "Respond to the call of God and the messenger," so the responsibility is placed on us, amidst the many things that call to us, to respond to the call of God and His messenger.

That the Prophet Muḥammad ﷺ calls us to "life," echoes the words of the Prophet ᶜIsā (Jesus) ﷺ, who described the purpose of his teaching in this way: "that you might have life and have it abundantly." Since answering the call of the prophets is no guarantee that one will live a longer life, it must be a spiritual life that is referred to here. "Life" is, after all, one of God's most beautiful names. It is a quality that turns mere material into something intelligent, responsive, capable of relationship. Responding to God's call, therefore, is what guides us to being more alive.

The human being is like a seed. A seed has no energy of its own, but it can respond. Every form of life has a capacity for response but none so much as the human being. In an infertile environment this capacity for response may be dormant. The cultivation we need to provide is through conscious awareness. This makes the difference between nominally being alive and being alive abundantly. With awareness we can develop all our faculties. The body, mind, spirit, and ecology form an interconnected whole. When a harmonious relationship exists among all of these, we have abundant life.

Ḥikmah: حكمة Wisdom. A conventional definition from the Oxford dictionary would be: *the capacity of judging rightly in matters of life and conduct.* From its Quranic context (see **Al-Ḥakīm**), *ḥikmah* is related to judging and discerning and also to judgment and law (*ḥukm*). So, to be wise is to understand the innate lawfulness of life, to know that certain actions produce certain results. The word *Ḥakīm* is also used to mean a doctor or healer, as well as a judge. And so this word "wisdom" is a deep understanding of causes and effects, the lawfulness within nature and within spirituality, as well. This is one of the foremost examples of the wisdom inherent in the Arabic of the Qur'ān and how it can shed light on such an essential subject.

Ḥikmah is also frequently paired with "the Book," *Al-Kitāb*. Both were sent down in the process of Revelation: *We gave the people of Abraham the Book and the Wisdom* (*Sūrah an-Nisā'* 4:54) and *Do not treat Allāh's signs lightly and remember Allāh's blessings to you, and that He sent down to you the Book and the Wisdom for your instruction, and be mindful of God, and know that God knows all things* (*Sūrah al-Baqarah* 2:231).

Himmah: همة Spiritual resolve. *Himmah* is the power of the heart awakened through intense spiritual intention or resolve. *Himmah* harmonizes all our faculties and desires in our striving toward Truth, Reality, Allāh. This is a quality that the sincere possess and which helps to overcome its opposite, *al-ḥiss*, the force of distraction, the inner noise which is ever more present today as a result of many factors. See ***Niyah:*** Intention.

Ḥirabāh: حرابة Terrorism, unholy war. Those who wage it are *muḥāribūn*. Often we hear in the media, the terms *jihād* and *jihād*-ists, applied to terrorists who kill innocent people. They are actually *muḥāribūn*, and their action would better be called *ḥirabāh*, a serious crime within traditional Islām—war aginst society. Anyone who kills wantonly someone they don't even know, and spreads chaos and fear within society is guilty of *fasād fi al-arḍ*, spreading corruption on earth.

Hū: هو The pronoun of Divine Presence, the indwelling presence of God. *Hū* is simply the third-person, masculine pronoun "he" in Arabic, but it has come to have special meaning in spiritual discourse, signifying the Divine Presence, which is especially present to the God-conscious human being.

Ḥukm: حكم Law. See: ***Ḥikmah.***

ᶜĪbādah: عبادة Worship (*ᶜabd*, worshipper, servant). In its narrower definition, worship (*ᶜibādah*) corresponds to religious rituals which are the expression of our surrender to God. In *Fiqh*, Islamic jurisprudence, worship is distinguished from actions (*muᶜāmalāt*). In a wider sense, worship is an expression of loving respect for a higher spiritual Power; a yearning found in human beings.

> *And I have created the invisible beings and human beings only that they may worship Me. No sustenance do I require of them nor do I require that they should feed Me. For God is the Giver of All Sustenance, the Lord of All Power, the Eternally Steadfast.* (*Sūrah adh-Dhāriyāt* 51:56-58)

When it is said "there are no gods but God," it implies that we shall worship the only God, that we shall recognize the Beneficent Reality behind the forms and events of our lives.

Idolatry, in any form, is a fundamental sin, that which separates us from the Real. Our idolatries include ambition, greed, misplaced sexual desire, the compulsive needs for intoxication and stimulation, and the need for attention. Whatever commands our attention is our master.

Whatever we worship consciously or unconsciously is what we serve. When we make an idol of the self, we increase self-will, self-justification, self-righteousness, and self-indulgence.

If we value something more than Spirit it is because of a misapprehension, a narrowness of vision. If we are identified with our small, partial self, we will be captured in the net of desires. If we are identified with Spirit, our desires will be in harmony the Divine Will.

"Worship" in its original sense means to value, to consider something worthy. The word is associated mainly with religious acts, and especially with those performed by some religious authority. In reality, however, every person who prays, who makes a call to the Divine, is performing an act of worship.

Human beings have an innate need to be in contact and communication with the Divine and to express themselves in loving respect and even awe. Through so much of human history worship was the means of contact with something of greater value, beauty, or power, but today worship in the true spiritual sense seems to be challenged by a multitude of distractions.

Worship in the form of crude idolatry, however, is very much alive, especially through sports and entertainments. A subtler idolatry exists in the worship of the self.

Of all the human activities, worship, provided it is with conscious presence, is the most direct route toward contact with the Divine. Worship in communion with sincere seekers and lovers of God is even more fruitful than worship alone. Worship that includes the whole of us—body, emotions, mind, and Heart—is more effective than worship which only includes a part of us. *Ṣalāt*, the ritual prayer of Islām, is such a complete activation of our human faculties, focusing them on the Divine.

Islamic tradition has also recognized a form of spontaneous prayer known as *duᶜāᶜ* in which the worshipper addresses the Divine either through a memorized supplication or spontaneously in one's own words. *Duᶜāᶜ* can lead to an inner activation, a deep recollection in which we make a sincere and specific call to Allāh, asking for the qualities and strengths we need to serve better in life.

Iblīs: إبليس The figure of Iblīs in Islām is similar to that of Satan in

Christianity. Although Iblīs was an angelic being, his vision couldn't penetrate the outward form of a thing in order to apprehend its inward meaning. When Ādam (the first human) was created, God commanded Iblīs and all the other angels to prostrate themselves before Ādam. Iblīs refused to bow down to this new creation of God. He reasoned to himself that he was superior to Ādam since he was made of fire while Ādam was only made of clay. In this one act of defiance Iblīs introduced the sins of pride, envy, and disobedience into the world. When confronted by God, Iblīs refused to take any responsibility for his sins; instead he accused God of leading him astray.

Iḥsān: إحسان Beautiful righteousness, doing something well and with quality for God's sake alone. Whereas Justice (*ᶜAdl*) requires that we give what is due, *Iḥsān* is giving even more than what is due. It is a generosity of virtue. The Prophet ﷺ said, "*Iḥsān* is that you worship God as if you saw Him; for even if you do not see Him, He sees you." We can strive to live life as if we could see God in front of us, or at least be continually aware that we *are seen*.

To develop as a human being in the vertical (or spiritual) dimension, we must learn to concentrate our will, awareness, mind, and feelings on actions that are in harmony with the standards of truth, i.e., aware of spiritual values and the Divine Presence.

Ijtihād: إجتهاد The continuing effort to apply Islamic principles. When there is not a precedent (*taqlīd*) in the Qurʾān or *Sunnah*, and when no direct analogy (*qiyās*) applies, *ijtihād* is called for. For nearly nine centuries, however, many legal scholars, believing that all issues have been addressed and nothing new can possibly arise, have taught that "the doors of *ijtihād* are closed." This assumption is beginning to be questioned more and more, and some scholars today believe that the Islamic world is in need of re-energizing a discussion of the issues facing Muslims in today's world. *Ijtihād* is derived from the verb *jahada*. Although the exact word *ijtihād* is not found in the Qurʾān, the principle of continual personal effort is a central concept in Islamic spirituality.

The word entered the Islamic vocabulary when the Prophet ﷺ asked

Muᶜādh, who was to govern a certain region, how he would make decisions. He replied: "According to the Qurʾān."

"And then what?"

"According to your example (*sunnah*)."

"And if you still don't find the answer?"

"Then I will make a personal effort (*ijtihād*)."

And this the Prophet approved.

Ilhām: إلهام Inspiration. The inspiration and guidance that come to anyone, as distinguished from *wahy* and *tanzil*, the revelations received by the Prophets.

ᶜIlm: علم Knowledge; science. Islām places a major emphasis on knowledge and its acquisition. The Prophet ﷺ said: "Seek knowledge even as far as China." There is more than one kind of knowledge, however. The highest knowledge is the knowledge that helps us to realize what it means to be a human being: the purpose of being human, our place in the universe, and our relationship with Absolute Truth, Allāh. The axioms of this knowledge are to be found in Revelation, and especially in the Holy Qurʾān. Next there is science, the practical knowledge of the empirical worlds. Islām, unlike some religious systems, has always supported the development of science. From its earliest days Islamic civilization placed a high value on scientific knowledge and became the collector and preserver of knowledge from other great civilizations: Greek, Indian, Chinese.

There is another category of knowledge which might be called mere speculation or conjecture: *Aẓ-ẓinn*, as it is called in Arabic. It is the kind of thinking, often based on some element of truth, that builds shaky edifices of interpretation through analogical reasoning or incomplete theories. Much of what passes for knowledge in our contemporary universities—including much of modern psychology, economics, and the social sciences, in general—falls into this category. At its weakest, it is an ever-changing labyrinth of conjecture that becomes fashionable, popular, and even dogmatic, until it is superceded by the next academic trend. One example of *aẓ-ẓinn* is "scientism," the belief that only what is empirically verifiable is "real." *They enjoy speculation and speculation is of no avail with the Real.* (*Sūrah an-Najm* 53:28)

There are many *āyāt* and *aḥādīth* affirming that the seeking of knowledge is essential to Islamic faith. Knowledge and knowing is mentioned in nearly a thousand different contexts in the Qur'ān.

> *Know that this Revelation is sent down with the knowledge of God. (Sūrah Hūd* 11:14*)*

> *Say, O my Sustainer, increase me in knowledge. (Sūrah Ṭā Hā* 20:114*)*

> *God will raise up the levels of those of you who have faith and who have been granted knowledge. And God is well acquainted with all you do. (Sūrah al-Mujādalah* 58:11*)*

Kāfūr ibn Qayṣ reported:

While Abū Dardā', one of the most beloved companions of the Prophet, was in Damascus, a man came from Medina to see him. He asked the man what was the purpose of his coming to Damascus. The man said: "I wish to check a tradition that I heard you had reported from the Prophet."

"Is that all you came for? You have no other business here?"

The man said "No. I came to hear you confirm what you heard from the Prophet."

Then Abū Dardā' said to the man: "Without any doubt, I heard the Messenger of Allāh say: 'Allāh leads to Paradise the one who travels far seeking knowledge. The angels spread their wings under his feet for him to tread upon. All that is in heaven and on earth, even the creatures in the sea, beg God for the forgiveness of the sins of the one who seeks knowledge. The superiority of the one who knows over the faithful who spend their time in prayer is like the brilliance of the moon over the stars. There is no doubt that the wise holders of knowledge are the inheritors of the prophets, for the prophets did not leave gold and silver as their legacy, but left knowledge. Whoever received from this inheritance is certainly the richest.'" (Abū Dā'ūd, Tirmidhī)

ʿAbdullāh ibn ʿUmar said that he heard the Messenger of Allāh say: "The best of worship for the faithful is to know what is right and what is wrong, with the intention of applying it in their lives. And the best of piety is to avoid that which is doubtful." (Ṭabaranī)

ʿAbdullāh ibn ʿUmar also reported that the Prophet ﷺ said: "Even a little knowledge is better than a lot of worship." (Ṭabaranī)

Abū ʿUmamah reported that the Prophet said: "On the Day of Judgment the pious person is told to enter Paradise, but the holder of knowledge is commanded to stay, to intercede for humankind." (Isfahani)

ʿAbdullāh ibn ʿUmar reported that he heard the Prophet say: "A man of knowledge is seventy times better than a pious man, and each of the seventy levels is as wide as the distance covered by a fast horse in seventy years." (Isfahani)

Abū Hurayrah reported that the Prophet said: "There is no greater worship in the opinion of God than the knowledge of one's religion. A scholar is a warrior against evil, and his strength is a thousand times greater than that of the pious. Everything has a support that holds it. The support of this religion is the people of knowledge." (Bayhaqī)

Abū Hurayrah also reported: "An hour spent in the evening to study the fundamentals of my religion is better than praying the whole Night of Power." (Bayhaqī)

Abū ʿUmamah reported: "Somebody asked the Prophet about a very devout, pious man and about a man of knowledge. The Prophet said: "The superiority of the man of knowledge over the pious man is like my state as compared to the worst of you. Certainly God and His angels, and all the inhabitants if this world and the heavens—unto the very ant in its hole and the fishes in the sea—pray and ask forgiveness for the one who seeks knowledge to teach humanity to do what is right." (Tirmidhī)

ʿUthmān ibn ʿAffān reported that the Prophet said: "On the Day of Judgment, first the prophets, then the holders of knowledge, and then the martyrs will intercede for humankind." (Ibn Mājah)

Muʿādh reported that the Messenger of Allāh ordered the Muslims: "Learn! For seeking knowledge is worship, and to seek knowledge for God's sake is a sign that you love and fear Him. To exchange knowledge with others is to praise God. To inspire people to learn is to struggle in God's way. To teach is the best way of giving alms. To be generous in imparting knowledge brings one close to God. (Ibn ʿAbdul-Barr)

Īmān: إيمان Faith. Faith is our certainty regarding the reality of the Unseen Beneficence from which comes a sense of peace and security.

Amānah is to create a condition of peace and security for someone. *Amānat* is something which is entrusted to someone. A *muᶜmin* is someone who can be trusted and relied upon.

The Qurʾān says: *It is not goodness (birra) to turn your faces towards East or West, but goodness is to 'āmana (to accept, have confidence in, be faithful to, and rely upon) God, the angels, the Book, and the prophets* (*Sūrah al-Baqarah* 2:177).

The Qurʾān again and again couples faith with a certain quality of action: "And those who keep the faith and do the actions of righteousness" *wa ʾāmanu wa ᶜamul uṣ-ṣāliḥāt.* Faith and action form a reciprocal relationship; the one strengthens the other. We cannot claim to have faith and not be willing to risk loss and even failure in the name of faith.

Faith can be understood as hope substantiated by knowledge and experience. We develop such faith (*īmān*) through a process of verification. Faith is understood to have an aspect of knowledge—it is not blind faith, but a knowledge confirmed by the heart which we can then rely upon. *He has inscribed faith upon their hearts.* (*Sūrah al-Mujādalah* 58:22) Because the spiritual reality is obvious neither to the senses nor to the intellect, it is a knowledge attained through the subtle faculties of the heart.

In the Qurʾān (as well as in the Gospels) we are called to a state of faithfulness. Unfortunately, both the Arabic word *īmān* and the Greek word *pistis* have too often been translated as "belief." It has too often been said that it takes faith to believe in God, that the facts that we have cannot add up to a certainty of God, and that to believe in God is an act of faith. In other words, belief in God, or Spirit, is not justified by the facts alone.

Most religions require belief in certain articles of faith and a verbal profession of faith. Catholics, for instance, must believe that Jesus is both a human being like us and also fully God. Muslims are asked to believe in the Day of Resurrection, in angels, and that the Qurʾān is the word of God. In these cases faith can mean the profession of a belief. But let us be quite clear and call this "superficial faith." Rumi says, "Beliefs vary from one religion to another, but faith is everywhere the same."

The effect that derives from the root or principle of faith is suggested by the word "faithful." It does not necessarily suggest belief in any doctrine. To be faithful is to have a single reference point. The lover will be faithful to the beloved. The mother will be faithful to her family. Jesus rebuked his disciples for not having faith. Even the disciples of Jesus could be said to be without real faith, and the word used to describe them was "perverse," a word that suggests a turning in different directions in confusion. The Qur'ān puts it this way: *Put your trust in Allāh and Allāh is sufficient as a Trustee. God has not assigned to anyone two hearts within his breast.* (*Sūrah al-Aḥzāb* 33:3–4) The implication here is that the way to wholeness and a unified sense of self is through the heart.

To have faith means that we have a center, an axis, a single point of reference. And yet this center, this point of reference, is not necessarily apparent from the start; it is not automatically possessed. On the contrary, the development of this faith will face many hazards and doubts, because we are pulled in so many directions, and we are so easily distracted.

For something to become or be a center for us it must in some way be magnetic. The strongest, most magnetic reference point is within us. This connection to Allāh, the ground of Being, is essentially good and beautiful. We find and explore that connection by focusing our awareness through the Heart, and in this way we come into contact with *Rūḥ*, Spirit.

The human being suffers from his own incompleteness. He or she suffers from being a fragment and being fragmented to the extent that he or she feels lonely, dependent, afraid, in conflict with himself, and subject to desires that must be controlled. He is grasping, clutching, and yearning most of the time.

As we know, the original meaning of *healing* was to make whole. The human being can be healed of separateness through contact with something whole. A person can know she is not separate from the whole. She can know the universe through knowing herself. This is a statement of faith, or hope substantiated by knowledge.

Traditionally, faith has been the step following repentance. If we repent of our incompleteness, of the unending desires of the *nafs* (ego), if we recognize our need for wholeness—that is the beginning of faith. Not until we sufficiently recognize our need can we be faithful and obedient to our own highest possibility.

Once we have this kind of faith (even if we possess as little as a mustard seed of it), we can begin to practice with constancy—whether cleaning windows or polishing the mirror of the heart. Then we can be said to be one of the faithful, a *mu*ᶜ*min*.

Already we have come rather far from the notion of faith as belief in doctrine. We can take a step further and say that faith is a truly creative function. Isn't it said that with faith all things are possible? And if two people join together in faith, the effect will be more than double. How is it that faith is creative?

Suppose that an individual has a certain quantity of psychic energy available to him during his lifetime, or during a single day for that matter. He has this quantity of psychic energy that is being spent continually in all the trivial interests, petty anxieties and titillations, excitements and disappointments that life brings. If he could bring his own being into a greater state of order and harmony, so that he could participate fully in what life brings and yet not suffer needless anxieties and distractions, and if he were to order his life around a single value of magnetic power, the power of higher Being, it would not be surprising if such a person had an unusual power of thought and feeling. If we make all our cares into a single care—the care for being tangibly in contact with the source of Life—that Life, that Creative Power, will attend to all our cares.

Insān: إنسان Human Being. A vehicle for individualized Spirit; the human is the most complete witness of Spirit within this material world. *Insān*, human-ness, is related to two roots: *nas*, meaning forgetful, and *ins*, meaning companionable, or intimate. Thus the human being has these two distinctive qualities: actual heedlessness and a potential capacity for great intimacy. The ultimate destiny of the human being is intimacy with God.

Al-Insān al-Kāmil: الإنسان The Complete, or Perfected, Human Being. *Al Insān al-Kāmil* has reached a harmony between the self (*nafs*) and God. Such a person can express and reflect the Divine Attributes appropriately and comprehensively because the self, being in submission, provides no resistance.

Islām: إسلام 1. The state of being surrendered to God. 2. The religion of the community of Muḥammad. There is an *Islām* which is the initial surrender to the precepts of religion, and there is an ultimate *Islām* which is the state of total surrender to God.

The Bedouin say, "We have attained to faith." Say [unto them, O Muḥammad]: "You have not [yet] attained to faith; you should [rather] say, 'We have [outwardly] surrendered'—for [true] faith has not yet entered your hearts. (*Sūrah al-Ḥujurāt* 49:14) The Bedouins of that time were so preoccupied with the pride of descent and tribal affiliations that their outward submission did not necessarily contain the inward state of faith and true surrender.

Islām, or true submission, is the universal state of nature, but for the human being it must be a conscious choice. *Do they seek something other than the religion of God? While all in the heaven and earth submit, willingly or unwillingly, bow before His will, and to Him all will be brought back. . . . If anyone desires a religion other than submission, it will never be accepted from him, and in the hereafter he will be among those at loss.* (*Sūrah Āl ᶜImrān* 3:83, 85)

Here are the range of meanings that can be associated with the root S-L-M. *Sallama* means to be purified of all defects, see, for instance *Sūrah al-Baqarah* 2:71 that refers to the cow that is perfect and without any defect. *As-Silm* (*Sūrah al-Baqarah* 2:208) means one who lives with peace and order and also maintains peace and order. *Tasalamat-il-Khailu* means horses that move in step. *As-silmu wa as-salamu* means to be obedient, to bow, to surrender. *Istaslama sakamat-tarīq* means one who walks in the middle of the path and does not deviate from it. *Qalū salama* means one who leads or takes up the middle path, to adopt a balanced way, avoid indecency, and practice humility. *As-salimatu* is a woman who is beautiful and in perfect proportion. All of these meanings add up to peace, order, purity, balance, moderation, and beauty.

Islām, in its ideal form, would be a way of life in harmony with the Divine Reality, in which human beings align themselves with the highest truth and apply it to the conditions of life. The conditions then established would reflect God's justice, mercy, generosity, and love. Anything that is essentially harmful to human beings or results in cruelty, anything which offends human dignity, could not, then, be considered Islamic.

Istikhārah: إستخارة Praying for a vision. (See section 2) c) v) in "Truth and Knowledge" on Visionary Dreams, *ar-Ruᶜyā aṣ-Ṣāliḥa.*)

Kabīr ibn ᶜAbdullāh is quoted as saying "The Prophet ﷺ taught us about dreaming in relation to the deeds that we do (how to get information through dreams regarding things we will do, or have done, or what our situation is.) He addressed us, 'When one of you intends to do something, let him do two *rakᶜāts* of prayer in addition to the obligatory number of *rakᶜāts*, and then let him or her recite:

My Allah, I ask for goodness according to what You know to be good for me, and I ask for strength from Your own strength. I ask for abundance because Your strength is sufficient for everything and my strength is not. You know everything; I don't know; it is You who know perfectly all that which is hidden. My Allah! If this (thing I intend) is good for my religion, and my life, and if the consequences of my deed will be good according to Your knowledge, make it easy for me to accomplish and make it fruitful, otherwise if You know this endeavor is not good for my religion, and my life, and that the consequences of this endeavor would be harmful, turn it away from me, and turn me away from it. Give me what is good for me and make me accept it.'"[27]

Jaḥīm: جحيم Hell. The root meaning of this word is to "block" or "prevent." Our sins block the development of the human being and cause it to regress. The object of life is continual spiritual development. Life is like a flowing stream which should not be impeded; the moment it is blocked, it becomes stagnant.

The Holy Qurʾān has used *Al-Jaḥīm* in the meaning of *Jahannam* (*Sūrah ad-Dukhān* 44:47, *Sūrah aṣ-Ṣaffāt* 37:55, 64, 68). The Qurʾān has also described the result of misdeeds as the torturing fire. In other words, we are burned by our own bad deeds.

If a person's life is led in harmony with Truth, which implies being in accord with one's own inherent nature (*fiṭrah*), then its latent potenti-

---

[27] Tirmidhī, pp. 202-203, *ḥadīth* 380.

alities are developed in such a way that it is enabled to continue progressing from one stage to the next. But if the potentialities are not developed, it does not have the energy to continue its development. This place of stoppage is called *Al-Jaḥīm* in the Qur'ānic concept.

Jahannam and Jannāh: جهنم و جنة Hell and Heaven. *Jahannam*, though usually translated as Hell, does not properly convey the *Qur'ānic* sense of the term. *Jahannam* is a Hebrew compound made up of *Ji* and *Hinnum*, meaning the valley of Hinnum. Gehenna was a famous valley south of Jerusalem where some say human beings were burnt alive and offered as sacrifices to the idol of Moloch. *Jahannam*, therefore, denotes a situation in which humanity is ruined.

According to the Holy Qur'ān, life is not limited to this world; it continues beyond death. The higher form of life that an individual with a developed soul is capable of leading after his life in this material world, is called a heavenly life, or the life of *Jannāh*. On the other hand, the evolution of a not-so-developed soul is bound to be thwarted—this kind of life is called an infernal life or the life of *Jahannam*.

Jannāh and *Jahannam* do not stand for places or localities; rather, they denote different conditions of human life which have been described metaphorically. It should also be clear that these conditions do not relate entirely to the life hereafter; they have their beginnings here in this world. A social order based upon Qur'ānic foundations results in a happy situation: the necessities of life are available in abundance and are secured in decent ways befitting the human dignity. This brings in a real happiness and peace of mind. This is called a heavenly life (*Jannāh*). On the other hand, a society based upon principles that contradict our innate human nature (*fiṭrah*) brings anxiety and discontent, and this is an infernal or Hellish life (*Jahannam*).

Muḥammad Asad offers these reflections on the chastisement of Hell and the dimensions of God's Mercy: *He will say: "The fire shall be your abode, therein to abide—unless God wills it otherwise." Verily, your Sustainer is wise, all-knowing* (*Sūrah al-Anʿām* 6:128). In reference to "unless God wills it otherwise," that is to say, unless He graces them with His mercy. Some of the great Muslim theologians conclude from the above and from the similar phrase in 11:107, as well as from several well-authenticated sayings of the Prophet, that—contrary to the bliss of paradise, which will be of unlimited duration—the suffering of the sinners in the life to come will be limited by God's mercy.

Behold, they who are lost in sin shall abide in the suffering of hell (*Sūrah Zukhruf* 43:74), i.e., for an unspecified period. In accordance with the Qur'ānic statement, "God has willed upon Himself the law of grace and mercy" (6:12 and 6:54)—the otherworldly suffering described as "hell" will not be of unlimited duration. Among the theologians who hold this view is Rāzī, who stresses in his comments on the above passage that the expression "they shall abide (*khālidūn*) in the suffering of hell" indicates only an indeterminate duration, but "does *not* convey the meaning of perpetuity." (Asad, *Sūrah al-An'ām* 6:128 note 114, *Sūrah Zukhruf* 43:74 note 53)

Jamal and Jalāl: جمال و جلال Beauty and Power; the two fundamental categories of qualities. Jalāl signifies the Divine Power which inspires awe. Jamal is the Divine Beauty which, when it overwhelms the heart, produces the experience of Divine Intimacy (*uns*).

Jihād: جهاد Striving in the way of God. The complete commitment of all one's faculties and resources toward personal or social transformation.

The idea of striving does not become prominent until the Medinan period, when the Qur'ān frequently refers to *those who have faith, have emigrated, and have struggled in the Way of God* (*Sūrah al-Anfāl* 8:74). Only after the Prophet and his community had been driven from their homes and lost everything they owned, was permission given to take up arms:

And fight in God's cause against those who wage war against you, but do not commit aggression—for verily, God does not love aggressors. And slay them wherever you may come upon them, and drive them away from wherever they drove you away—for oppression (fitnah) is even worse than killing. (*Sūrah al-Baqarah* 2:190-191) Muḥammad Asad comments: "This and the following verses lay down unequivocally that only self-defence (in the widest sense of the word) makes war permissible for Muslims. Most of the commentators agree in that the expression *lā ta'tadū* signifies, in this context, 'do not commit aggression'; while by *al-mu*ᶜ*tadīn* 'those who commit aggression' are meant. The defensive character of a fight "in God's cause"—that is, in the cause of the ethical principles ordained by God—is, moreover, self-evident in the reference to 'those who wage war against you,' and has been still further clarified in 22:39 —'permission [to fight] is given to those against whom war is being wrongfully waged'—which, according to all available Traditions, constitutes the earliest (and therefore fundamental) Qurʾanic reference to the question of *jihād*, or holy war (see Ṭabarī and Ibn Kathīr in their commentaries on 22:39). That this early, fundamental principle of self-defence as the only possible justification of war has been maintained throughout the Qurʾān is evident from 60:8, as well as from the concluding sentence of 4:91, both of which belong to a later period than the above verse." (Asad, *Sūrah al-Baqarah* 2:190 note 167)

Jihād, however, is not primarily armed struggle. Rather its primary meaning, based on a *ḥadīth*, is to struggle with oneself: 1. The "greater *Jihād*" is the struggle with egoism. 2. The "lesser *Jihād*" is the struggle for human rights, which sometimes requires fighting.

Strive in God's Way with your possessions and your selves. (*Sūrah at-Tawbah* 9:41)

Seek the means to come to Him and strive in His way (*Sūrah al-Māᶜidah* 5:35)

And God has preferred those who strive. (*Sūrah an-Nisāᶜ* 4:95)

In the history of Islām, *jihād* also became a *modus operandi* for expanding the Islamic empire, extending it into the *dār al-ḥarb,* the non-Islamic territories, or so-called abode of war. It should be clearly understood that conversion by means of the sword has always been against Islamic Law. In the conquered territories, people could accept Islām, or accept the protection of Islām as a religious minority, in which case they would be allowed to live according to their own revealed scriptures and religious law.

Kāfir: كافر Denier, misbeliever. Although this word is often translated as "unbeliever," as if to imply that it means the rejection of a specific religious doctrine, the word cannot properly be associated with "belief," as such. A belief implies mental acceptance of something as true, whether such belief is based on experience, indoctrination, or authority. Beliefs are essentially mental concepts which then exercise a power over the emotions.

The *kāfir* is not necessarily the denier of a "belief" but someone who denies the reality of a spiritual dimension of existence, who does not recognize nor trust that there is a beneficent and purposeful order. The "denier" places trust in material existence and the human self alone.

The Arabic word *kāfir* has two primary meanings: first, to cover or hide, and thus to cover the spiritual reality; and second, to be ungrateful. The habitual denial of the spiritual dimension of life leads to a preoccupation with things and with one's own self. The complex of attitudes and judgments that proceed from this state may actually reduce the sensitivity of the heart and thus affect the quality of relationships.

Today it is customary to say that someone is "in denial" when they refuse to admit, for instance, that they are addicted to something like alcohol, for instance. The denier (*kāfir*) is the one "in denial," one who has turned his or her back on reality and pursues unreality instead.

The denier is not necessarily one who disbelieves in Islām, since there are faithful people (*muʿminūn*) in other faith traditions. Worse yet is to call a fellow Muslim a *kāfir* because of a disagreement over religious matters.

According to Muḥammad Asad: In the Qurʾān such people are spoken of as having *Hearts with which they fail to grasp the truth, and eyes with which they fail to see, and ears with which they fail to hear* (*Sūrah al-Aʿrāf* 7:179). The meaning of this term in the earliest portions of the Qurʾān revealed indicates that the meaning of this term was determined by the meaning which it had in the speech of the Arabs before the advent of the Prophet Muḥammad ﷺ. That being so, *kāfir* cannot be simply equated with "unbeliever" or "infidel" in the specific, restricted sense of one who rejects the system of doctrine and law promulgated in the Qurʾān and amplified by the teachings of the Prophet; it must have a wider, more general meaning. This meaning is easily grasped when we bear in mind that the root verb is *kafara*, "he (or it) covered (a thing)." In 57:20, the tiller of the soil is called *kāfir* without any pejorative implication, meaning "one who covers", i.e., the sown seed with earth, just as the night is spoken of as having "covered" (*kafara*) the earth with darkness. In their abstract sense, both the verb and the nouns derived from it have a connotation of "concealing" something that exists or "denying" something that is true. Hence in the rest of the Qur'ān, other than 57:20 just cited, a *kāfir* is "one who denies (or refuses to acknowledge) the truth" in the widest, spiritual sense of this latter term; that is, irrespective of whether it relates to a cognition of the supreme truth—namely, the existence of God—or to a doctrine or ordinance enunciated in the divine writ, or to a self-evident moral proposition, or to an acknowledgment of, and therefore gratitude for, favors received. (Asad, *Sūrah al-Baqarah* 2:6 note 6; *Sūrah al-Muddaththir* 74:8 note 4)

Kalām: كلام Scholastic theology (literally, speech).

Karīm: كريم Generosity, nobility. The first revelation to Muḥammad, what would become *Sūrah al-ᶜAlaq* of the Qur'ān begins with the affirmation of a generous relationship between the Divine and the human. *Read in the name of your Sustainer who created. Created the human being from a "clinging substance" (ᶜalaq). Read, for truly your Sustainer is the Most Generous* (*Sūrah al-ᶜAlaq* 96:1-3). And so began the process of the transmission of knowledge which is the greatest evidence of God's Mercy and Generosity, the revelation which calls itself: *the speech of a noble messenger* (*Sūrah al-Ḥāqqah* 69:40).

Furthermore, in the Qur'ān the human being is described not as essentially sinful, but as a creature of dignity: *We have honored the children of Ādam and carried them on land and sea* (*Sūrah al-Isrāᶜ* 17:70). And the essential criterion of honor and nobility is not ancestral lineage, religious hierarchy, or even intellectual accomplishment; the criterion of nobility is mindfulness of the Divine (*taqwā*): *The noblest among you in the sight of God is the one most conscious of God.* (*Sūrah al-Ḥujurāt* 49:13)

Khalīfah: خليفة Successor; representative of God upon the earth. The linguistic meaning here is "to take the place of, to succeed, to come after." The true human being who has fulfilled the purpose of his life is God's *Khalīfah*. It is through such a human that the Divine Attributes can manifest fully on earth. In the Holy Qur'ān: *I am setting upon the earth a*

Representative (*Sūrah al-Baqarah* 2:30), and . . . *appoints you to be representatives upon the earth* (*Sūrah an-Naml* 27:62).

Khuluq: خلق Character; habit of behavior. *And you (Muḥammad) are on an exalted standard of character* (*Sūrah al-Qalam* 68:4). *Akhlāq*. the plural form, refers to the virtues that comprise good character in Islamic moral teachings.

According to a ḥadīth: "The most perfect in faith among the faithful are the most perfect in conduct. A person can cross great distances with good conduct that he cannot cross with worship and adoration." (Al-Bukhārī, "*Ādāb*," 95; Muslim, "*Zakāt*," 142.)

However, *akhlāq* also refers to the unconscious, habitual behaviors of people. When the ancient Prophet Hūd tried to warn the people of ᶜ*Ād* of the consequences of their unbridled greed, saying *Heed me and be mindful of God,* their response was: *This is nothing but the customs (akhlāq) of the ancients and we are not ones to worry about punishment* (*Sūrah ash-Shu*ᶜ*arā*ᶜ 26:137). Unless *khuluq*, character, is qualified by the attributes of God, it is merely the habit of behavior.

Kufr: كفر Denial, misbelief. See ***Kāfir***.

Kun: كن Be! *He is the Originator of the heavens and the earth and He only needs to say to a thing "Be" and it is* (*Sūrah al-Baqarah* 2:117). *His Being alone is such that when He wills a thing to be, He only needs to say to it, "Be!" and it is* (*Sūrah Yā Sīn* 36:82). This is how the Absolute brings things out of His Being into existence. In Islamic metaphysics, everything that exists in the material world is a sign, or symbol, of a higher level of Being. Everything in existence can be traced back to that One Being who is the Originator of all. The word *kawn*, the universe, is a verbal noun derived from the imperative, *Kun*.

Malā*ᶜ*ika: ملائكة (see **Angel**)

Maqām: مقام See: **Hal.**

Maẓhar: مظهر A symbol. From the verb *aẓhara*, to disclose or cause to appear. A symbol is an apparently finite thing that points toward something that's unbounded and indescribable. The knowledge conveyed by the symbol cannot be apprehended in any other way, nor can the symbol ever be explained once and for all.

The verb *aẓhara*—which has the root meaning to shine forth, be radiant, as in *Al-Aẓhar*—appears in *Sūrah aṣ-Ṣaff* 61:9 and the following: *He it is who sent His Prophet with the guidance and the religion of truth to the end that it will shine forth over all religion; and Allāh suffices as a witness* (*Sūrah al-Fatḥ* 48:28). Unfortunately it has been misunderstood and mistranslated to mean to "prevail over" or "dominate" all religions. It is enough that Islām shed light upon and be an example to other religions.

Minhāj: منهاج Way of life; literally: an open road. *Unto every one of you have We appointed a law (shirʾah) and way of life (minhāj). And if God had so willed, He could surely have made you all one single community: but [He willed it otherwise] in order to test you by means of what He has vouchsafed unto you.*[28] *Vie, then, with one another in doing good works! Unto God you all must return; and then He will make you truly understand all that on which you were wont to differ.* (*Sūrah al-Māʿidah* 5:48)

Mīzān: ميزان Measure, balance, scales. From the verb *wazana*, "to weigh." One of the responsibilities of the human being as *Khalīfah* of God is to maintain the cosmic harmony and equilibrium within creation. Thus God has offered revelations to guide us: *God has sent down the Book with the Truth and the Balance.* (*Sūrah ash-Shūrā* 42:17)

Each of us also bears responsibility for our actions, and the scales, *mīzān*, are a symbol for our eternal accountability. *Fill up the measure and the balance with justice* (*Sūrah al-Anʿām* 6:152).

Muʿmin: مؤمن A person with faith (*īmān*). See: ***Īmān.***

---

[28] I.e., "in order to test, by means of the various religious laws imposed on you, your willingness to surrender yourselves to God and to obey Him" (Zamakhsharī, Rāzī), "and thus to enable you to grow, spiritually and socially, in accordance with the God-willed law of evolution" (*Manār* VI, 418 f.). (Asad, *Sūrah al-Māʿidah* 5:48, note 67)

Murāqabah: مراقبة Being observant. See **Meditation.**

Murīd: مريد The Disciple, the one who is willing.
Murad: مراد The one who is willed. See: **Will.**

Mushrik: مشرك Idolator, associator. Someone who offers his adoration to anything besides the one God. Hence polytheists and idolators are "associators." However on a more subtle level, anyone who adores God with an impure love is an associator. too. For instance someone who adores God, not for His Self alone, but in expectation of some other reward, is also an associator. See: ***Shirk.***

Nabī: نبي See: **Prophet.**

Nafs: نفس See: **Self.**

Niyyah: نية Intention. The Prophet Muḥammad ﷺ said, "Actions are of value according to their intention." Niyyah is an aim or wish, clearly formulated in conscious words or thought, by which we mobilize the energy to attain that aim or wish. Having a spiritual intention, which counters distraction, temptation, and straying, is the beginning of integrity.

Qalb: قلب Heart. The subconscious/supraconscious faculty of mind through which spiritual realities are made intelligible to the human being. The heart is the core of our individuality and the mid-point between self (*nafs*) and Spirit (*Rūḥ*), which allows a connection to be formed between them. In other words, the heart is the threshold between the material world of existence and the spiritual world.

He has inscribed faith upon their hearts (*Sūrah al-Mujādalah* 58:22), and, at the same time, *Indeed, in the remembrance of God hearts find rest* (*Sūrah ar-Raᶜd* 13:28). According to a *ḥadīth qudsī*: *The heavens and the earth cannot contain Me; only the heart of my faithful servant can contain me.*

Qiblah: قبلة Orientation; facing the *Kaᶜbah* in Mecca, the unifying direction toward which the Muslim faithful orient themselves in their prayers.

In the Qur'ānic System, the visible symbol is the *Kaᶜbah* about which the Qur'ān says, *The first house built for humanity (the Kaᶜbah) is in Bakkah which provides guidance to entire humanity* (*Sūrah Āl ᶜImrān* 3:95) and *anyone who enters here, has attained security* (*Sūrah Āl ᶜImrān* 3:96). The *Kaᶜbah* is an empty cube; if one were to place oneself in its center, one would be in actuality at the point where all Muslims in the world face each other.

Ar-Rabb: الرب Sustainer, Lord. The root meaning of this word is to nurture, educate, bring to perfection. This is the function the Divine serves for all of creation. Allāh is the *Rabb al-ᶜĀlamīn*, the Sustainer of the Universes. This process of nurturing is called *Rabubiyyat*. In the Qur'ān Moses says: *Our Rabb is He who gave to each thing its form and nature and then guided them.* (*Sūrah Ṭā Hā* 20:50)

Ar-Rabb is related primarily to the manifestation of the Divine Names or Attributes. Allāh cannot be known or experienced directly. However, Allāh wishes to be known and experienced by His creation. So He imposes limits upon Himself in order to reveal His attributes as the created world. A particular Attribute of God can assume the form of a personal Rabb for a particular person. For one, it might be *ar-Raḥmān*; for another, *al-ᶜAdl*, the Just; for another, *al-Wadud*, the All-Loving. Through a unique devotional bond to his own *Rabb*, the individual human being may come to know the sum of God's Attributes or Names and thereby gain a fuller understanding of the Divinity.

Rabitah: رابطة A bond that strengthens. An affectionate bond formed between a student and teacher in which spiritual support and protection is maintained.

Raḥmah: رحمة Mercy, blessing, grace. Although impossible to capture in a single word, this is the fundamental quality that God offers His creation. The root of this word means "womb," that through which God's beneficence acts to allow and protect the development of life itself. This beneficence never ends, overseeing every stage of growth for every human being that is receptive to it, and indeed for all of existence.

And when those who believe in Our messages come unto thee, say: "Peace be upon you. Your Sustainer has willed upon Himself the law of grace and mercy (raḥmah)." So that if any of you does a bad deed out of ignorance, and thereafter repents and lives righteously, He shall be [found] much-forgiving, a dispenser of mercy (raḥim)." (*Sūrah al-Anʿām* 6:54) There are only two places (*Sūrah al-Anʿām* 6:12 and *Sūrah al-Anʿām* 6:54) where the expression "God has willed upon Himself as a law" (*kataba 'alā nafsihi*) occurs, and in both instances it refers to *raḥmah*; none of the other divine attributes has been similarly described. This exceptional quality of God's compassion and mercy is further stressed in *Sūrah al-Aʿrāf* 7:156: *My Mercy overspreads everything,* and finds an echo in the authentic Tradition of the Prophet in which God says of Himself, "Verily, My Mercy outstrips My Wrath" (Bukhārī and Muslim).

Ar-Raḥmān: الرحمن The Most Compassionate, or the Most Gracious. *Say: "Invoke God, or invoke the Most Compassionate: by whichever name you invoke Him, His are all the attributes of perfection* (*Sūrah al-Isrāʿ* 17:110). According to Muḥammad Asad, the epithet *ar-Raḥmān* has an intensive significance, denoting the unconditional, all-embracing quality and exercise of grace and mercy. It always appears with the definite article and is applied exclusively to God.

Ar-Raḥīm: الرحيم The Merciful. This word occurs almost always following either *ar-Raḥmān* or *al-Ghafūr*, the Forgiving. One of the few occasions when it stand alone is *Sūrah al-Fatḥ* 48:29: *Muḥammad is God's Messenger and those who are with him are firm and unyielding toward all deniers of the truth, yet full of mercy toward one another . . . . This is their parable in the Torah as well as in the Gospel: they are like a seed that brings forth its shoot, and then He strengthens it, so that it grows stout, and stands firm upon its stem, delighting the sowers.*

While *ar-Raḥmān,* the All-Compassionate, rains down grace upon all of existence, the All-Merciful, *ar-Raḥīm,* is the blessing found in every condition of life when we turn consciously back to God.

The following extremely well-authenticated saying of the Prophet is an example of God's ultimate Mercy: "[On the Day of Judgment,] those who deserve paradise will enter paradise, and those who deserve the fire, the fire. Thereupon God, the Sublimely Exalted, will say, "Take out [of the fire] everyone in whose heart there was as much of faith [or, in some versions, "as much of good"] as a grain of mustard seed!" And so they will be taken out of it, already blackened, and will be thrown into the River of Life; and then they will come to life [lit., "sprout"] as a herb sprouts by the side of a stream: and did you not see how it comes out, yellow and budding?" (Bukhārī, on the authority of Abū Saᶜīd al-Khudrī, in *Kitāb al-Īmān* and *Kitāb Badᵓ al-Khalq*; also Muslim, Nasāᵓī and Ibn Ḥanbal.)

Rasūl: **رسول See Prophet.**

Ribā: ربا Usury; profit on money that is lent. From the root *rabā,* to grow. The basic idea of Islamic economics and justice is that a person will receive and benefit only from what he strives or works for (*Sūrah an-Najm* 53:39). Passive earning from the mere lending of capital is forbidden. *O you who keep the faith, do not consume usury, whether doubled or multiplied, but be mindful of God that you may truly prosper* (*Sūrah Āl ᶜImrān* 3:130).

One can partner with someone, sharing in the profit or loss of a business venture, but to lend and demand interest whether someone succeeds or fails is not considered just. If fastidiously avoided, a society free of usury would result in a situation free of the dominating power of capital. In a society with no restraints on capital, however, capital tends to increase itself without regard for human well-being. Capital will automatically flow to those money-making ventures, whether they are beneficial to society or not. In the Islamic framework, a person with a great amount of capital is obliged to find people or businesses to partner with and cannot merely put money into an interest-bearing account. This involves people in the realistic exchange of capital with all the mutual responsibilities and relationships this entails. In recent times, the subject of *ribā* has been contested—some scholars, for instance, suggesting that mortgages involving interest can actually benefit the mortgage holder and help to increase their wealth. *Ribā,* however, as out-and-out usury that enslaves people to high interest rates has been condemned not only by Islām, but in the past by Christianity as well.

Rūḥ: روح Spirit. The first or primary manifestation of God. *Rūḥ* is what God breathed into Ādam (*Sūrah al-Ḥijr* 15:29), and into Mary, making her pregnant (*Sūrah al-Anbiyāᶜ* 21:91; *Sūrah at-Taḥrīm* 66:12). It is what Jesus was strengthened with by God (*Sūrah al-Baqarah* 2:253). Spirit is the essence of life itself. Spirit as an attribute of the human being is described as an impulse or directive (*amr*) from God (*Sūrah al-Isrāᶜ* 17:85).

Rūḥ is one of the three primary aspects of human individuality. It is the very center of the center of our being. At the opposite pole there is self (*nafs*). Between these two poles is heart (*qalb*) which potentially is the bridge between Spirit and self. *Rūḥ* is our direct connection with the divine. It is like a non-dimensional point which offers access to the realm of Unity and the Divine Attributes, or Names.

Saḥābah: صحابة Companions. These were the people who were closest to the Prophet during his lifetime. It is interesting to note that they were not called followers or students, but companions, stressing the essentially egalitarian and intimate spirit of early Islām.

Ṣalaḥa: صلح To be righteous, to do a deed of righteousness. ***Ṣaliḥ:*** Harmonious, reconciling. a harmonious action; from *aṣlaḥa*, to reconcile, to put in perfect order, harmony, or symmetry.

This word is often coupled with faith in the Qurʾān, reminding us that faith and action go hand in hand. The "goodness" of *ṣaliḥat* consists in its reconciling power. *Aṣlaḥ-alaihi* means to remove another person's defect and to establish beauty and balance. *Aṣ-Ṣulḥu* means attaining mutual peace and reconciliation.

Ṣalāt: صلاة The ritual prayer of Islām. Human beings are enjoined in the Qurʾān to "establish (or perform) *Ṣalāh*." In *Sūrah al-Baqarah* 2:3 are mentioned *those who keep faith with the Unseen, establish Ṣalāh, and share with others out of what we have provided.*

The faithful are enjoined to serve God and to perform the prayer in remembrance (*Sūrah Ṭā Hā* 20:14) and to be watchful over one's prayers (*Sūrah al-Baqarah* 2:238).

Aṣ-Ṣamad: الصمد The Eternal, Independent Being. This term occurs in the Qurʾān only once, and is applied to God alone. According to Muḥammad Asad it comprises the concepts of Primary Cause and eternal, independent Being, combined with the idea that everything existing or conceivable goes back to Him as its source and is, therefore, dependent on Him for its beginning as well as for its continued existence.

Sirr: سر Secret. Spirit, the innermost essence of the human being, an individual's center of consciousness; the source of an individual's being. At this mysterious point, the individual comes into contact with that which is Holy. This knowledge helps the human being to discern the Real from the illusory.

Shahādah: شهادة The testimony of faith: *Ashadu an lā ilāha ill-Āllah, wa ashadu anna Muḥammadan rasūlullāh.* As it come from the verb *shahida*, which has the double meaning to both perceive and to testify to what one perceives, this might be translated as "I witness and testify that there is no god but God, and I witness and testify that Muḥammad is the Prophet of God."

Shahīd: شهيد Witness, martyr. The ***Shahīd*** is, above all, the one who witnesses and testifies to the reality of the Divine. While the primary meaning is a "witness," the word has also been applied to those who die in a just battle, and even those who die in tragic circumstances such as a car accident.

Shaikh or shaykh: شيخ Spiritual guide or teacher. In the spiritual, as opposed to the political context, a *shaikh* is a saintly, mature individual who serves as a spiritual guide for others. The *shaikh's* words provide some guidance, but even more benefit comes from simply associating with an individual who has attained such purity of heart, for it reflects something of God's perfection. Through proximity to the *shaikh*, the disciple's own Heart is strengthened and gains the upper hand in its spiritual combat with the ego.

Of course not everyone who claims to be a *shaikh* really is spiritually developed, and a great deal of spiritual harm is inflicted on the disciples of so-called *shaikhs* who actually are self-serving. In order to distinguish the charlatans from the saints, the potential disciple must already have purified his heart to some extent. If the disciple's ego still dominates his intellect and heart, he will tend to be drawn to these charlatans, and their influence will help his ego to become even stronger. In contrast, an individual who has already acquired some humility and made progress in virtue will be able to recognize the genuine saint.

A female spiritual guide is a *shaikha*.

Shayṭān: شيطان An evil spirit or inclination; a Satan. The root meaning is from *shaṭana* which means to be far away, or to be contrary, or rebellious. In the Qur'ān, the Prophet Abraham ﷺ says, *O my father! Do not worship Satan—for, verily, Satan is a rebel against the Most Gracious!* (*Sūrah Maryam* 19:44)

According to Muḥammad Asad: The absurdity inherent in the attribution of divine qualities to anything or anyone but God is here declared, by implication, to be equivalent to "worshipping" the epitome of unreason and ingratitude symbolized in Satan's rebellion against his Creator. In this connection it should be noted that the term *shayṭān* is derived from the verb *shaṭana*, signifying "he was [or "became"] remote [from the truth]" (*Lisān al-ᶜArab*, *Tāj al-ᶜArūs*); hence, the Qur'ān describes every impulse that inherently offends against truth, reason, and morality as "satanic," and every conscious act of submission to such satanic influences as a "worship of Satan." (*Sūrah Maryam* 19:44, note 33)

Sharīᶜah: شريعة Sacred Law. A code of living based upon the Qur'ān and the example (*sunnah*) of Muḥammad, whose intention is to restore and safeguard our human well-being and to preserve the best conditions in the social order.

From the verb: *sharaᶜa*, "to ordain, to lay down a law." The word literally means "an open, clear way" and occurs once in the Qur'ān: *We set you upon an open way (sharīᶜah) of direction* (*amr*) (*Sūrah al-Jāthiyah* 45:18). Another variant is used in the Qur'ān:

Unto every one of you have We appointed a [different] law (shirᶜah) and way of life. And if God had so willed, He could surely have made you all one single community: but [He willed it otherwise] in order to test you by means of what He has vouchsafed unto you.[29] *Vie, then, with one another in doing good works! Unto God you all must return; and then He will make you truly understand all that on which you were wont to differ.* (*Sūrah al-Mā*ᶜ*idah* 5:48) Thus, the Qur᾿ān addresses all who believe in God—Muslims and non-Muslims alike—that the differences in their religious practices should make them strive to excel one another in doing good rather than lose themselves in mutual hostility.

According to Muḥammad Asad, the expression "every one of you" denotes the various communities of which mankind is composed. The term *shir*ᶜ*ah* (or *sharī*ᶜ*ah*) signifies, literally, "the way to a watering-place" (from which men and animals derive the element indispensable to their life), and is used in the Qur᾿ān to denote a system of law necessary for a community's social and spiritual welfare. The term *minhāj*, on the other hand, denotes an "open road," usually in an abstract sense: that is, "a way of life." The terms *shir*ᶜ*ah* and *minhāj* are more restricted in their meaning than the term *dīn*, which comprises not merely the laws relating to a particular religion but also the basic, unchanging spiritual truths which, according to the Qur᾿ān, have been preached by every one of God's apostles, while the particular body of laws (*shir*ᶜ*ah* or *sharī*ᶜ*ah*) promulgated through them, and the way of life (*minhāj*) recommended by them, varied in accordance with the exigencies of the time and of each community's cultural development. This "unity in diversity" is frequently stressed in the Qur᾿ān (e.g., in the first sentence of 2:148, in 21:92-93, or in 23:52 ff.). (*Sūrah al-Mā*ᶜ*idah* 5:48 note 66)

Shirk: شرك the ascribing of divinity to anything beside God; the state of being idolatrous of our own ego, or of some other power. It was first applied to the pagans of Mecca who preferred to worship their idols rather than to hear the message of Muḥammad. *Shirk* literally means "associating," i.e., associating other forces with an independent power,

---

[29] I.e., "in order to test, by means of the various religious laws imposed on you, your willingness to surrender yourselves to God and to obey Him" (Zamakhsharī, Rāzī), "and thus to enable you to grow, spiritually and socially, in accordance with the God-willed law of evolution" (*Manār* VI, 418 f.). (Asad, note 67)

equal to God. Expressed another way, whenever we lose sight of God's power over all things and assign that power to apparent phenomena, we are guilty of *shirk. Whoever associates anything with God has gone far astray* (*Sūrah an-Nisāʿ* 4:116).

The Islamic teaching is that Muḥammad was the last Prophet, the last human being to have brought a divinely-revealed Book. His mission was to confirm the truth of previous revelations to humanity, theoretically recognizing the possibility that countless messengers had come to earth with essentially the same message. After him, however, there would be no need for further revelations, although God would never cease to guide and inspire the hearts of human beings. The process of historical revelation was complete and no more religions or moral codes needed to be introduced.

According to Muḥammad Asad: Because of the universal applicability and textual incorruptibility of its teachings—as well as of the fact that the Prophet Muḥammad ﷺ is "the seal of all prophets," i.e., the last of them (see 33:40)—the Qurʾān represents the culminating point of all revelation and offers the final, perfect way to spiritual fulfillment. This uniqueness of the Qurʾanic message does not, however, preclude all adherents of earlier faiths from attaining to God's grace: for—as the Qurʾān so often points out—those among them who believe uncompromisingly in the One God and the Day of Judgment (i.e., in individual moral responsibility) and live righteously "need have no fear, and neither shall they grieve." (*Sūrah al-Māʿidah* 5:48 note 66)

The most blatant *shirk* is to divinize another human being, a religious hierarchy, or a man-made dogma. At various times, emperors, kings, and dictators have claimed virtual absolute authority over people, erecting monuments to themselves, forcing their own image into the center of public life. There have also been religious leaders who claimed to be gods, or who presented their own false teachings as divinely revealed truth.

The more subtle shirk is taking our own ego for a god and submitting to its demands. Among the false gods that we human beings have falsely worshipped are power, authority, physical image, status, and wealth. The Qurʾān says: *And worship God [alone], and do not ascribe divin-*

ity, in any way, to anything beside Him. (*Sūrah Āl ʿImrān* 3:64) The expression *shayʾan* (here rendered as "in any way") makes it clear that *shirk* is not confined to a worship of other "deities," but implies also the attribution of divine or quasi-divine powers to persons or objects not explicitly regarded as deities but serving, nevertheless, to cause human beings to unduly rely on them. If we assign even to a prophet or saint some magical power, we are confusing and corrupting the pure simplicity of trust in God which is at the heart of the Qurʾānic revelation.

On the other hand, when we properly honor Muḥammad, or other prophets and saints, we honor them for their closeness to God. The Prophet ﷺ said, "Shall I tell you who are the best among you?" They replied, "Yes, O Messenger of God!" He told them, "The best among you are those who, when seen, remind one of God." (Ibn Mājah)

Shūrā: شورى Mutual consultation. More than 1,400 years ago, at the time when despots and kings ruled the world, the Qurʾān directed the Muslims to decide their affairs by mutual consultations (*Sūrah al-Ḥajj* 22:36).

And remember that whatever you are given now is but for the passing enjoyment of life in this world—whereas that which is with God is far better and more enduring. It shall be given to all who attain to faith and in their Sustainer place their trust; and who shun the more heinous sins and abominations; and who, whenever they are moved to anger, readily forgive; and who respond to the call of their Sustainer and are constant in prayer; and whose rule [in all matters of common concern] is consultation among themselves; and who spend on others out of what We provide for them as sustenance; and who, whenever tyranny afflicts them, defend themselves. (*Sūrah ash-Shūrā* 42:36-39) This particular qualification of true believers—regarded by the Prophet's companions as so important that they always referred to this *sūrah* by the key-word "consultation" (*shūrā*)—has a double import: firstly, it is meant to remind all followers of the Qurʾān that they must remain united within one single community (*ummah*); and secondly, it lays down the principle that all their communal business *must* be transacted in mutual consultation. (Asad, *Sūrah ash-Shūrā* 42:38 note 38)

Ṣifāt: صفات Attributes, Qualities, and Names (*asmā*ᵓ) of God that are the real causative factors of the manifestation of material existence. Everything in existence is a manifestation of a single Source, Allāh, who is revealed through His attributes. As we see the budding of flowers in spring we recognize *Al-Khāliq*, the Creator, or *Al-Laṭīf*, the Subtle, and *Al-Muṣawwir*, the Bestower of Form. When we see the power of a great storm or an earthquake, we recognize and remember *Al-ᶜAziz*, the Mighty, and *Al-Jabbār*, the Compeller. When we view the incredible balance within the ecology of nature we may recognize *Ar-Razzāq*, the Provider, and *Al-Wahhāb*, the Bestower, and *Al- Muḥyī*, the Giver of Life, and *Aṣ-Ṣabūr*, the Patient.

Each Name can be thought of as a bi-unity: an uncreated quality and a created expression or servant. These two roles are forever distinct. The uncreated quality may be thought of as the *Angel* or the *eternal substance* or the *eternal individuality* of a given individual's being. The created individual or servant is seen as a manifested, or epiphanized form of the uncreated quality. As God is indivisible, all of the divine Names are said to be in sympathetic union with one another, yet each Name embodies a unique attribute of the Divine. Unlike other divine Names, Allāh is the Name which is invested with the sum of all the divine Attributes. See: ***Asmā*ᵓ**.

Sunnah: سنة Customary practice, example, or way. This terms has two major usages in the Islamic context:

1. In the earliest days of Islām, *sunnah* referred primarily to the customary practice that was current among the Muslims themselves. In time, however, the term became restricted to the example of the Prophet Muḥammad's own words and actions, what he approved or disapproved of, his manners and practices.

The Qurᵓān does not explicitly describe some of its directives such as, for instance, the form of the ritual prayer (*ṣalāh*). Much of Islamic practice is derived from the *Sunnah* of Muḥammad. The Qurᵓān says: *You have a good model in God's Messenger* (*Sūrah al-Aḥzāb* 33:21).

The *Sunnah* also supplemented the Qurᵓān in the formulation of the principles of Islamic Law, *uṣūl al-fiqh*.

The *Sunnah* is also divided into those principles applying to worship and morals: *as-sunnah muʾakkadah,* which have a virtually obligatory character, and those more elective matters of behavior: *as-sunnah az-zāʾidah.* In this latter category, for instance, the eminent jurist, Ibn Ḥanbal, declined to eat watermelon because he was not aware of any situation in which the Prophet ate watermelon. Nevertheless, many of the Prophet's minute behaviors, such as stepping into a room with the right foot first, indicate a degree of consciousness and intentionality which, if emulated, would help human beings develop a high degree of mindfulness, respect, and dignity.

2. In the Qurʾān, *sunnah* refers primarily to the "ways" of God, indicating the lawful justice that has always existed: The good will be rewarded and the evil will incur eternal accountability. *Such was the sunnah (practice) of God among those who lived in the past, and you will find no change in the sunnah of Allāh* (*Sūrah al-Aḥzāb* 33:62).

Tafakkur: **تفكر** Reflection. To reflect on things, ultimately seeing them in relationship to the Divine.

Malik Badri writes:

> *Tafakkur* does not have a precise English translation. It involves deep thinking, but it goes beyond the exclusively mental activity which the Western mind usually attributes to the "thinking" faculty. The words "contemplation" and "meditation," which are closest to the word *tafakkur* in meaning, are frequently used as synonyms in English dictionaries, although "meditation" often carries a spiritual connotation. However, the term "meditation" has so often been used in relation to the spiritual practice of eastern religions that its use to explain *tafakkur* can be misleading, especially when it is used to describe types of meditation which are associated with the pursuit of altered states of consciousness and which are held to transcend more "sober" styles of thinking. It is for this reason that it may be more appropriate to translate it as "contemplation" rather than "meditation." *Tafakkur* is a cognitive spiritual activity in which the rational mind, emotion and spirit must be combined. Essentially,

it is a refined form of Islamic worship, in which we verify the truth of revelation and approach nearer to God through the contemplation of His signs in the created universe.

There are indeed signs for all who are endowed with insight, and who remember God standing, and sitting, and when they lie down to sleep, and reflect upon the creation of the heavens and the earth (*Sūrah Āl ᶜImrān* 3:190-191).

Soon we will show them our signs in the utmost horizons of the universe and within their own souls until it becomes manifest to them that this revelation is indeed the truth (*Sūrah Fuṣṣilat* 41:53).[30]

Tanzīl: تنزيل Revelation. (Literally, "what is sent down.") *Truly this is a revelation (tanzil) from the Sustainer of the Universes, sent down (nazala) with the Spirit upon your heart so that you may notify them in the clear Arabic language.* (*Sūrah ash-Shuᶜarāᶜ* 26:192-195)

Tanzīh: تنزيه Transcendence; Incomparability. From nūzhat which signifies something without any imperfection. This refers to the aspect of the Divine which is utterly transcendent and bears no relation to anything in existence. It is balanced, however by *tashbīḥ*, which is God's similarity to created things by which His attributes are reflected in the creation. See also: ***Tashbīḥ***.

Taqwā: تقوى Mindfulness of God; God-consciousness (Asad). To be aware of the possible negative consequences of our actions and thus to be vigilant and conscious of God. "The noblest, most honorable for you in the sight of God is the one who is most advanced in *taqwā*." (49:13)

This would be one of the foremost attributes of a true Muslim. It would be hard to find an adequate translation of this word in any language. Its root meaning is to guard oneself. In its limited sense, *taqwā* is

---

[30] Revised, abridged and expanded from *Contemplation: An Islamic Psychospiritual Study*, by Malik Badri. The International Institute of Islamic Thought, Herndon, VA, USA, 2000, page xiv.

fastidiousness in following the divine law and refraining not only from any acts that are forbidden, but even from permissible actions that might lead to the risk of the greater sins. The Messenger of God, Muḥammad, said:

> It is possible for one who does doubtful things to commit forbidden acts, just as it is possible for the flock of a shepherd pasturing near a field belonging to another to wander into that other field. Know that each ruler has a private area under his protection; the private area of God is the area of what has been forbidden. Also know that there is a part of our flesh which, if it is healthy, the whole body will be healthy, And if it is ailing, the whole body will be ailing. This is the heart.

Taqwā is guarding ourselves from whatever is spiritually negative or harmful. *Taqwā*, however, should not be conceived in a negative way, or as a negative state. It is a kind of positive fear—not a fear of punishment but of doing harm, either to others or ourselves. *Taqwā* is like the feeling of responsibility and vigilance one would feel if you were entrusted with the care of an infant. You would do everything possible to see that the infant was safe and out of harm's way.

Taqwā is a quality of consciousness which considers the consequences of our actions, including the less obvious consequences of our feeling and thoughts. A person living in *taqwā* actually has the pleasure of a good conscience and the assurance that God is pleased with him or her.

> *And make provision for yourselves – but, verily, the best of all provisions is God-consciousness (taqwā): remain, then, conscious of Me, O you who are endowed with insight!* (*Sūrah al-Baqarah* 2:198)

> *Help one another in furthering virtue and God-consciousness (taqwā), and do not help one another in furthering evil and enmity; and remain conscious of God.* (*Sūrah al-Mā*ᶜ*idah* 5:2)

> *We have bestowed upon you from on high [the knowledge of making] garments to cover your nakedness, and as a thing of beauty: but the garment of God-consciousness (taqwā) is the best of all.* (*Sūrah al-A*ᶜ*rāf* 7:26)

Ṭarīqah: طريقة The Spiritual path. ***Ṭarīqah*** is a lineage tracing back to a founder who reached a high degree of spiritual attainment, and who is their link in a chain of transmission going back to the Prophet Muḥammad ﷺ. Participation in a *ṭarīqah* usually involves initiation, or "taking hand" with a mentor, acceptance of a disciplined practice in addition to the fundamental practices of *sharīʿah*, and participation in the community life. Islamic tradition recognizes *ṭarīqah* as one of four levels of the spiritual life: *sharīʿah, ṭarīqah, maʿrifah, ḥaqīqah.* Each of these levels—the sacred law, the spiritual path, gnosis, and realization of Truth—builds upon and incorporates the previous level.

Tashbīḥ: تشبيه Similarity to God; the Divine as immanent in the world. According to a *ḥadīth* transmitted by Ibn Ḥanbal, Ādam was made in God's image. The similarity between Allāh and His creation consists in the sharing of the Divine Names. All of creation is a manifestation of God's names, and thus the Divine is immanent in the world. *Tashbīḥ* is contrasted to *tanzīh*: God's incomparability and transcendence.

Tawakkul: توكل Reliance upon God. Authentic trust in God develops from knowing that there is only One Trustee, *Al-Wakīl*, worthy of our trust, and turning all our affairs over to that One. *Whoever puts his trust in God, God will be sufficient for him* (*Sūrah aṭ-Ṭalāq* 65:3); *And therefore let those who trust place all their trust in God* (*Sūrah Ibrāhīm* 14:13).

Tawbah: توبة Repentance. It literally means "turning back" and in reference to repentance it is a turning toward the Real, back to our Source, which is God.

Tawḥīd: توحيد Unity, Oneness. This is a central doctrine of Islām. All levels of existence, all metaphysical planes of reality form a unity, because everything takes its existence from the One Being, Allāh. All opposites are held within this Unity. This truth is expressed in the phrase "There is no power nor strength except with God": *wa la hawla wa la quwwata illa billah.*

Taʿwīl: تأويل Interpretation of the Qurʾān, often in allegorical or symbolic terms. Literally it means to trace something back to its origin. It is generally of a more inward and metaphorical nature than the other mode of interpretation known as *tafsīr*, which is usually concerned with linguistic, contextual, and historical understanding. From an orthodox point of view, a *taʾwīl* interpretation should never contradict the outer and apparent exoteric sense of the text. *Taʾwīl* can lead to theophanic vision, a way of seeing reality in which everything seen takes on symbolic meanings.

Umm: أم Literally "mother," and by extension: source, foundation. The Milky Way Galaxy is called the *Umm-an-Najūm*. *Umm-ar-Raʾss* means the brain, a center where all the things unite. *Umm-ul-Qurā* means the mother of cities—*Makkah (Mecca)*. *Umm-ul-Kitāb* means the archetypal source of all revelation, including the prototype of the Holy Qurʾān.

Ummī: أمي Unlettered, illiterate (literally in the condition of a new-born). This is from the same root as *ummah*. The *Qurʾān* has addressed Arabs as *Ummiyūn* which means a nation which was not previously been given any Scripture (*Sūrah Āl ʿImrān* 3:20). In *āyāt Sūrah al-Baqarah* 2:78 and *Sūrah al-Jumuʿah* 62:2 *Ummiyūn* means people who were illiterate or unlettered.

Ummah: أمة Community or nation. According to Muḥammad Asad: A group of living beings having certain characteristics or circumstances in common, also meaning "people," "nation," "genus," "generation," "civilization," "cultural period," and so forth. One of the meanings of the term *ummah* is "people of one time" or "age"; another, "people of one kind," i.e., "a nation" or "a community." Taking into consideration a third, well-established meaning, namely "a particular way of life" or "of behavior," the term "community" comes, in this instance, close to the modern concept of "civilization" in its historical sense. (Asad, *Sūrah al-Anʿām* 6:38 note 30; *Sūrah al-Fāṭir* 35:24 note 18)

And had thy Sustainer so willed, He could surely have made all mankind one single community (ummah wāḥidah): but He willed it otherwise, and so they continue to hold divergent views (*Sūrah Hūd* 11:118). (See also 5:48 and

10:19-20.) The Qur'ān stresses once again that the unceasing differentiation in men's views and ideas is not incidental but represents a God-willed, basic factor of human existence. If God had willed that all human beings should be of one persuasion, all intellectual progress would have been ruled out, and "they would have been similar in their social life to the bees and the ants, while in their spiritual life they would have been like the angels *constrained* by their nature always to believe in what is true and always to obey God" (*Manār* XII, 193)—that is to say, devoid of that relative free will which enables man to choose between right and wrong and thus endows his life—in distinction from all other sentient beings—with a moral meaning and a unique spiritual potential. (Asad, *Sūrah Hūd* 11:118 note 150)

Wahm: وهم Delusion. Titus Burckhardt comments: "Some writers, including ʿAbd al-Karīm al-Jīlī, have said that the dark pole of the mind is *al-wahm,* a term which means conjecture and also opinion, suggestion, and suspicion, and so mental illusion. This is the reverse of the speculative freedom of the mind. The power of illusion of the mind is, as it were, fascinated by an abyss; it is attracted by every unexhausted negative possibility. When this power dominates the imagination, imagination becomes the greatest obstacle to spirituality. In this context may be quoted the saying of the Prophet ﷺ that 'the worst thing your soul suggests to you is suspicion.'[31]"

Waḥy: وحي Revelation (literally, to communicate instantaneously by sign). *He (Muḥammad) does not speak from some whim but from a revelation revealed* (*Sūrah an-Najm* 53:2-3).

This is also the word that is used in the following *āyah, And Your Sustainer revealed to the Bee* (*Sūrah an-Naḥl* 16:68). God instills the nature of every creation through *waḥy*. As Muḥammad Asad comments on this verse: The expression "He has inspired" (*awḥā*) is meant to bring out the wonderful quality of the instinct which enables the lowly insect to construct the geometrical masterpiece of a honeycomb out of perfectly-proportioned hexagonal, prismatic wax cells—a structure which is most

[31] *An Introduction to Sufism,* chapter 15, *The Intellectual Faculties*, pages 93-98.

economical, and therefore most rational, as regards space and material. Together with the subsequently mentioned transmutation, in the bee's body, of plant juices into honey, this provides a striking evidence of "God's ways" manifested in all nature. (*Sūrah an-Naḥl* 16:68 note 77)

Likewise the Qur'ān says: *We revealed ('awḥaynāa) to Moses' mother to suckle him* (*Sūrah al-Qaṣaṣ* 28:7). And another *āyāt* (*Sūrah Fuṣṣilat* 41:12) says, *He created seven orbs in two phases and communicated through waḥy ('awḥa) the destiny of every orb,* i.e., the unseen matrix that guides everything in the outer universe so that everything is fulfilling the task assigned to it. *Are you not aware how every creature in the heavens and earth extol His glory? Each knows how to worship and glorify Him.* (*Sūrah an-Nūr* 24:41)

Wajd: وجد Ecstasy; rapture. It comes from the root, *wajada,* "to find." The word for Being is *Wujūd.* So there is an implied connection that to find the true nature of what exists will result in an experience of ecstasy. The people of spiritual maturity assert, however, that a higher state is the sobriety capable of containing ecstasy. ʿAbd al-Qādir al-Jīlānī said: "*Wajd* is the holy plenitude of Spirit that results from invocation, and the holy plenitude of the soul, in communion with the Spirit."

Wajh: وجه Face. "Face" expresses personality, glory and majesty, inner being, essence, self, all the noble qualities which we associate with the Beautiful Names of God. *Wajh* means:

(1) Literally "face," but it may imply

(2) Countenance or favor, as in *Sūrah al-Layl* 92:17-21: *But those most devoted to Allāh shall be removed far from the Fire, those who spend their wealth for increase in self-purification, and have in their minds no favor from anyone for which a reward is expected in return, but only the desire to seek for the countenance of their Lord Most High, and soon will they attain satisfaction;*

(3) Honor, glory, Presence as applied to God, as in *Sūrah al-Baqarah* 2:115 *To Allāh belong the East and the West: wherever you turn, there is the Presence of Allāh. For Allāh is All-Pervading, All-Knowing;*

(4) Cause, for the sake of, as in *Sūrah al-Insān* 76:9: *We feed you for the sake of Allāh alone: no reward do we desire from you, nor thanks;*

(5) Nature, inner being, essence, self, as in *Sūrah al-Māʾidah* 5:111: *That they may give the evidence in its true nature and shape* and *Sūrah al-Qaṣaṣ*

28:88: *And do not call on another god besides God. There is no god but He. Everything is perishing except His Face. To Him belongs the Command, and to Him will you all return.*

Al-Wujūd: الوجود Being. On the one hand, *Wujūd* signifies what truly is. For some people, therefore this implies material existence, but from the spiritual point of view, God's existence or Being is more real than anything in the material creation, and all material things have derived their very existence from God's Being.

If Allāh is total and absolute potential, then Being is the first differentiation of Allāh which generates the creation of the world. Being, therefore, contains all the possibilities of existence in their perfect, unmanifest condition.

As far as the experience of the human being is concerned, Being is the timeless, spaceless attribute of the Divine, satisfying in and of itself, that can be experienced by the conscious soul. It is the Ocean as opposed to the foam (existence).

Within Being is a polarization of active and receptive, the Pen and the Preserved Tablet (*al lawḥ al-maḥfūẓ*), *yang* and *yin* in Chinese philosophy, *eidos* and *hyle* in Greek.

When we say that a particular person has or reflects "being," it suggests the kind of person who is aware of or connected with Being, or, in other words, identified with the reality of the Divine.

Our "level of being" is the degree of our identification with Spirit. Since it is our human destiny to encompass all levels, from the material, archetypal, angelic, and spiritual, the more a person has consciously integrated these levels of experience, the more he or she is a carrier of the power of Being. Spiritual emancipation, or liberation, is the release from all contingencies and circumstances into the freedom of pure Being. Salvation is being in harmony with Being.

Yaqīn: يقين Certainty. Certainty opens the gate to every kind of spiritual and human attainment. It has many degrees. A person with weak certainty is attached to changing circumstances and places his hope in them. A person with strong certainty acts in a clear and decisive way, yet knows that the outcome of his actions is in the hands of God. Success or failure, praise or blame, expansion or contraction are all greeted with equanimity when one's heart is focused on God.

"Even if the veil between the seen and the unseen were to lift, my certainty would not increase." (ʿAlī ibn Abī Ṭālib)

This term is used to express different levels of knowledge. *ʿIlm al-yaqīn* is the knowledge or certainty that comes from learning about something, as when you are told that Mecca, for instance, exists. *ʿAyn al-yaqīn* is the certainty that comes from experiencing or seeing something first hand, rather than just hearing about it, as when you visit Mecca. *Ḥaqq al-yaqīn* is the deepest certainty that comes from communion with the object of knowledge, as when you have lived in Mecca and understood many things that as a visitor you would not have known.

Zakāt: زكاة The annual "purifying charity" which is usually given directly to those in need; one of the Five Pillars of Islam. It is reckoned at one-fortieth of one's disposable wealth. It has two meanings: one is "growth," or "nourishment" as when a plant flourishes. The other meaning is "purification." So, to give *zakāh* is to help your own wealth grow, as if there were a spiritual law operating that wealth is increased by generosity. The second idea, is that what we give to those in need contributes to the purification of whatever wealth remains. These principles of generosity have served Muslim peoples well, limiting the hoarding that comes from fear of scarcity, and instilling the idea that the poor have a right to the general wealth and resources of the community as a whole.

Ẓulm: ظلم A transgression, sin; literally, something that is out of place. *Az-Ẓaʾlim* is someone who transgresses other people's rights, misappropriates, or causes disorder. A classic example of *ẓulm* would be "putting the fox in charge of the chicken house." This word is used hundreds of times in the Qurʾān, and its original meaning is to cause disorder, especially by going to excess, by disrupting the proper order, or by putting something in the wrong place.

In today's world, the expropriation of resources, the exploitation of labor, and the mishandling of power would be examples of *ẓulm*. Likewise, any behavior, emotion, or thought that distorts our essential humanity would be *ẓulm*. To be over-preoccupied with worldly accumulation, especially to the extent that one is led to deny the truth, is *ẓulm* against ourselves. *Behold, as for those who are bent on denying the truth, neither their worldly possessions nor their children will in the least avail them against God; and it is they who are destined for the fire, therein to abide. The parable of what they spend on the life of this world is that of an icy wind which smites the tillage of people who have sinned against themselves, and destroys it; for, it is not God who does them wrong, but it is they who are wronging themselves.* (*Sūrah Āl ʿImrān* 3:116–117)

Terms in English

THESE DEFINITIONS are offered to help create a consistent vocabulary for clearer spiritual and psychological communication. In the process of the education of the soul it is useful to infuse certain common terms with a meaning that can support the overall process. The word "effort," for instance, has the conventional meaning of using energy to get something done. In our glossary, effort describes the conscious, intentional action that overcomes inner resistance and helps to develop the capacities of the soul. It is related to the Arabic word *jahada*, to struggle, from which is derived the concept of *Jihād al-Akbar*, the inner struggle within the self to overcome unconsciousness and egoism.

It is also important to mention that some of the terms we use for psychological and spiritual realities are primarily descriptive. If we mention the "false self," it is not to suggest that there is a literal entity called the false self, but rather to describe an aspect of ourselves. If we mention "the commanding soul," "the repentant soul," or "the tranquil soul," for instance, it is not to suggest that there are three souls contained within man. Even the terms "soul" and "Spirit" are attempts to describe aspects of our experience and are not meant to be taken too literally, as absolute entities in themselves.

Nevertheless, this process of naming and describing with greater precision and intentionality is very important in our overall spiritual education. With such a vocabulary we may avoid misunderstanding, clarify our communication, and increase our understanding of ourselves and others.

Abrogation: The belief that certain verses of the Qur'an have been abrogated, i.e. superseded, by others. Those who hold this view take some of the verses we have already discussed, remove them from their context, interpret them in an absolutistic way, and, furthermore, claim that other Quranic verses that would clearly contradict these narrow and distorted interpretations have been abrogated. The justification for this theory of abrogation is this verse:

Any message which We annul or consign to oblivion We replace with a better or a similar one. Dost you not know that God has the power to will anything? (*Sūrah al-Baqarah* 2: 106)

This verse occurs in the middle of a passage addressing some of those people of earlier revelations, who strongly opposed the Muslims, primarily Christians and Jews, who wanted to hold exclusively to their own scriptures and refused to accept that the Qur'an could have been a legitimate bestowal from God. The verse immediately preceding this one says:

Neither those from among the followers of earlier revelation who are bent on denying the truth, nor those who ascribe divinity to other beings beside God, would like to see any good ever bestowed upon you from on high by your Sustainer; but God singles out for His grace whom He wills – for God is limitless in His great bounty. (*Sūrah al-Baqarah* 2:105)

Because the same word, ayat, is used for verses of the Qur'an as well as the messages of earlier revelations, the abrogationists would contend that God had reason to arbitrarily change revealed spiritual principles, i.e. to essentially rewrite the revelation as He went along. However, according to Muhammad Asad:

There does not exist a single reliable Tradition to the effect that the Prophet ever declared a verse of the Qurʾān to have been "abrogated." At the root of the so-called "doctrine of abrogation" may lie the inability of some of the early commentators to reconcile one Qurʾanic passage with another: a difficulty which was overcome by declaring that one of the verses in question had been "abrogated." This arbitrary procedure explains also why there is no unanimity whatsoever among the upholders of the "doctrine of abrogation" as to which, and how many, Qurʾān-verses have been affected by it; and, furthermore, as to whether this alleged abrogation implies a total elimination of the verse in question from the *context* of the Qurʾān, or only a cancellation of the specific ordinance or statement contained in it. In short, the "doctrine of abrogation" has no basis whatever in historical fact, and must be rejected. On the other hand, the apparent difficulty in interpreting the above Qurʾanic passage disappears immediately if the term *āyah* is understood, correctly, as "message," and if we read this verse in conjunction with the preceding one, which states that the Jews and the Christians refuse to accept any revelation which might supersede that of the Bible: for, if read in this way, the abrogation relates to the earlier divine messages and not to any part of the Qur᾿ān itself. (Footnote to *Sūrah al-Baqarah* 2:106)

Angel, Malak or Malᶜak, plural Malāᶜikah: ملاك، ملائكة In Arabic *malak* comes from *la᾿aka*, "to send on a mission." Ibn Mājah (born 209/824) says of them: "It is believed that angels are of simple substance, created of light, endowed with life, speech, and reason . . . . Know that the Angels are sanctified from carnal desire and the disturbance of anger; they never disobey God in what He has commanded of them, but do as they are commanded. Their food is the celebration of His glory; their drink is the proclaiming of His holiness; their conversation, the remembrance of God, whose name be exalted; their pleasure is His worship; and they are created with different forms and different powers."

One of the angels, Iblīs, refused to acknowledge the superiority of Ādam and became an enemy of humanity, seeking always to waylay us from our highest human potential. This symbolic story illustrates the satanic aspect of ego's pride which refuses to recognize the spiritual nature contained within Ādam's form.

Appropriateness: The quality of behavior which is the result of love and humbleness.

Attainment: The progress in developing and using our human faculties. Something can be considered an attainment if it can be produced at will.

Awareness: The faculty of perception. Awareness, however, is not necessarily a synonym for "consciousness." Consciousness is a more comprehensive state of presence which can include being conscious of what our attention (awareness) is drawn to. Awareness may include a simple sense perception such as hearing, while consciousness can include sensations, thoughts, and feelings simultaneously. As awareness develops and becomes more and more comprehensive, even to the degree of awareness being aware of itself, then we have "consciousness."

Beauty: Whatever pleases the senses, mind, and heart. True Beauty, however, draws us into relationship with the Divine. Whether it be the beauty of nature, the beauty of virtue or character, the beauty of anything, it is a reflection of that ultimate Beauty which is Divine: "God is beautiful and loves the beautiful" (*Ḥadīth Qudsī).*

Ultimately Beauty becomes our point of contact with Love. It is the degree of Spirit in anything that is its beauty. Sometimes we mistake glamor, the imitation of beauty, for real beauty. What is beauty, if it is not purity, radiance, depth?

Within our own heart we can discover Beauty. We may discover great beauty in contemplation and yet not consider that beauty as originating with ourselves. The qualities which a pure attention perceives are sometimes not qualities that we have known as our own. Love of Beauty, especially spiritual Beauty, connects us to Spirit. What we contemplate, we become.

This invisible beauty discovered within has a counterpart in the sensible world. The sensible world becomes beautiful to the extent that we are conscious of this invisible beauty within our being.

Beauty awakens a nostalgia that leads us beyond the world of appearances to new qualities contained within the heart. The qualities latent within our own hearts are Divine Attributes. It is because the Divine Compassion exists to reveal Itself to us, that there exists the possibility of knowing the Infinite by knowing ourselves.

Beloved: The metaphor of the Beloved has been widely used in Arabic, Persian, and Islamic poetry as a symbol for God. The metaphor of the Beloved, in this sense, is one's point of contact with Spirit (*Rūḥ*).

Compassion and Mercy, Raḥmān and Raḥīm: رحمن رحيم Both the divine epithets *Raḥmān* and *Raḥīm* are derived from the noun *raḥmāh,* which signifies "mercy," compassion," "loving tenderness" and, more comprehensively, "grace." From the very earliest times, Islamic scholars have endeavored to define the exact shades of meaning which differentiate the two terms. An explanations advanced by Ibn Qayyim (as quoted in *Manār* I, 48): the term *raḥmān* circumscribes the quality of abounding grace inherent in, and inseparable from, the concept of God's *Being*, whereas *raḥīm* expresses the manifestation of that grace in, and its effect upon, His creation—in other words, an aspect of His *activity*. (Asad, *Sūrah al-Fātiḥah* 1:1 note 1)

Say: "Unto whom belongs all that is in the heavens and on earth?" Say: "Unto God, who has willed upon Himself the law of grace and mercy" (*Sūrah al-An*ᶜ*ām* 6:12). The expression "God has willed upon Himself as a law" (*kataba* ᶜ*alā nafsihi*) occurs in the Qur'ān only twice, here and in verse 6:54, and in both instances with reference to His grace and mercy (*raḥmah*); none of the other divine attributes has been similarly described. This exceptional quality of God's grace and mercy is further stressed in 7:156: "My grace overspreads everything"—and finds an echo in the authentic Tradition in which, according to the Prophet ﷺ, God says of Himself, "Verily, My grace and mercy outstrips My wrath" (Bukhārī and Muslim). (Asad, *Sūrah al-An*ᶜ*ām* 6:12 note 10)

> *The Compassionate (ar-Raḥman) is sitting on the Throne (Asad: the Most Gracious, established on the throne of His almightiness) (Sūrah Ṭā Hā* 20:5*).*

Completion: The state of being fully aware of one's relationship with the Whole; realizing the Truth, *Al-Ḥaqq*, which is none other than *Allāh ar-Raḥmān*, God the infinitely Gracious. Completion, in this sense, is synonymous with perfection, as in *al-insān al-kāmil*, the "perfected human being."

Contentment, Qanū*ᶜ*: قنوع True contentment comes from gratitude and the awareness of one's present richness, without precluding the receiving of more.

Contemplation: To reflect on, to focus various faculties of the mind on a particular thing. Contemplation is a cognitive spiritual activity in which the rational mind, emotion, and spirit are combined. To contemplate the divine is to join ourselves—all our faculties—with the "template" of the Divine, and so to be potentially transformed by Divine Being.

Consciousness: A potentially comprehensive awareness that encompasses thinking, feeling, and bodily sensation without being limited by them. The degree of our awareness, inner and outer, on as many levels of our experience as are available to us. The awareness of oneself as a thinking, feeling, and doing human being.

The development of consciousness in this sense is the development of our humanness itself, the refining of our perceptions, and the development of our latent capacities. See also: **Awareness**.

Discipline: Methodical pursuit. The state of someone who does something for a purpose. The word discipline is related to disciple, which literally means student, one who is able to continue learning from everything, all the time.

Real discipline is the methodical pursuit of a conscious aim. If, for instance, one has the aim to become a first-rate soccer player or an accomplished author, one will bring all the activities of one's life into alignment with that aim. A *murīd*, in the spiritual sense, is one who has a quest and has applied his will (*irāda*) toward that quest.

Ecology: The relationship among living organisms and the environment, from the Greek *oikos*, house. A true *eco*nomy would include an awareness of the *eco*logy. Islamically, ecology is related to the notion of Oneness, *tawḥīd,* applied to our material and biological environment. The human being as *khalīfah* of God has an obligation to keep the balance, *al-Mīzān*. The Qur'ān speaks often about communities and societies that have ignored this balance and "spread corruption upon the earth."

Effort: The term is used here in the special sense of conscious, intentional action. Effort is one of the methods by which we can spiritualize the mind, or, in other words, create presence (*ḥuḍūr*) and develop our souls.

When we consider the subject of effort we must consider the forces of affirmation and denial that exist within each human being. Whenever we affirm something within ourselves through a real decision, we will inevitably bring into play a denying force, both within and without. If we affirm the wish to concentrate, we will encounter some distraction. If we affirm the wish to be active, we will encounter our passivity. If we decide to give, we will encounter that which withholds, and so forth.

We have within us a "yes" and a "no," and this is the basis of all effort. Something in us affirms and something else denies. As we know, the human being usually deals with his environment through personality, which consists of conditioning, acquired habits, likes and dislikes. But the human being also has an essential self with essence qualities like awareness, will, and love. This essential self is usually quite buried beneath our awareness and our personality. Personality has taken the authority and the initiative. We act on the basis of what "it" desires, what "it" affirms. If we can submit to the higher Self, however, essence can more and more become the affirming force in our lives, and the personality itself can be cultivated, brought into service.

Effort is not to be understood as the clash of opposites, but as the creation of a conscious presence, an awareness that we *are*, and this presence includes the awareness of the "yes and no" within us. This presence stands above the clash of all opposites, balancing both.

Without the existence of denial there can be no effort or "work," but the existence of denial allows us to generate the energies essential to work by giving us the reason, the friction, and the fire to affirm our presence on a higher level. The mechanism of like and dislike will always remain, but through our conscious relationship to it we awaken higher faculties in ourselves.

Ego, Nafs: نفس The self, the subjective experience of "I-ness," of being an individual self. The *nafs* is that which we will always continue to transform and develop into ever more subtle and spiritualized states of being. Traditional teaching offers seven levels in the development of transformation of the self.

Egoism: The self in its more compulsive manifestations, especially those motivated by selfishness: *an-nafs al-ʾammārah bis-sūu* (the self which commands evil). Egoism displays itself as self-righteousness, self-importance, self-will, etc. Egoism develops when the intellect, absorbed in selfishness, begins to promote itself at the expense of the whole self and especially the subtle faculties of the mind like the heart. Egoism is the effect of the joining of unconscious thought and selfish desire.

Elder: A mature carrier of the teaching; a light-holder of the tradition. There is a great need in society today that we value the experience and hard-won wisdom of our elders, especially those who have led a life of commitment and service.

Emancipation: Freedom from fear, especially from the fear of loss. The spiritual journey from beginning to end can be characterized as the overcoming of fear. A whole philosophy and methodology could be developed around this fact. Fear is the greatest obstacle standing between us and the abundant life we could know.

Epiphany: The manifestation or shining-forth of the Divine.

Essential Self: The soul, the being who we essentially are at our core. Our essence is our essential nature, that which is utilizably good in us. This essential self is not an absolute term but a relative term signifying that core self that we come to know as we become relatively free of the identifications with our social programming and conditioning. This essential self will be found to have the attributes of Spirit, including unconditional love and fundamental creativity.

Our post-industrial, materialistic, secularized culture does not encourage the awakening of our essential self. The widespread consumerism, the self-indulgence, the habits of immediate gratification, the moral relativity of our age, and the displacement of individual and communal responsibilities by large corporations, institutions, and bureaucracies bring us fewer moments of truth, fewer encounters with our essential and authentic selves. The distraction of entertainments that appeal to every human weakness and the pervasive artificiality that technologies have brought increase the difficulty of being what we are meant to be.

Essence: 1. God; that from which everything proceeds. 2. The essential nature of anything; that which is inherently and utilizably good in something.

False Self: An imaginary self that seeks to avoid disturbance, maximize pleasure, attract attention and approval. It is constructed within and defended by the mind. It is the source of the tendencies of greed, envy, jealousy, resentment, pride, and, ultimately, denial, *kufr*.

Somewhere, somehow, we began to live as if we were separate, alone, and in danger. We constructed a false self out of that fear and need for security, attention, and approval. We have been steadfastly defending it ever since. This false self exists in the intellect—in other words in our thoughts, and particularly those thoughts that have been generated by fear and the desires that fear creates. It has developed and come between our essential self and objective reality and causes us to live in a world of relative delusion. This totality of acquired fears, habits, preferences, and opinions must be exposed and understood.

When the false self proclaims independence and authority for the self, it divorces itself from the heart, or subconscious mind. As it begins to assert its own autonomy, it loses contact with its own source of integrity. The false self can be understood *as intellect struggling for its own survival at the expense of the whole mind.*

A fixation on the false, compulsive self can distort our sense of reality, of justice, of balance. Again and again this false self can ruin things for the *whole* of oneself. The real possibility of the moment is destroyed from too much self-importance as well as from too little self-respect, from greed as well as from indifference, from our disorderly desires as well as from inertia. Following the impulses of this false self, our essential self is more and more eclipsed.

We are slaves to a tyrant called "ego." Unless we are extremely astute, we do not see the extent to which we are controlled by our habits, compulsions, and desires, because we are working so hard to satisfy their random expectations.

The ego could be useful as a servant and a messenger, handling our affairs in the world according to the instructions and guidance it receives through the heart, from the essential self. But without spiritual presence and intention we may not be able to distinguish the guidance of the heart from the impulses of our egoism. Without awakening the will, we cannot understand what is really needed in any moment and act to fulfill it.

For this reason, various situations which require patience, humility, and service, and which reorient our awareness, are among the practices offered to those who have committed themselves to the Work of spiritual awakening. It may take special methods of effort and intention in order for this fixation on the false self to be brought into relief, but once seen and realized, our wish to awaken intensifies, and we never sleep as easily again.

The work to become free of the false self which covers the essential self is accomplished through loving but objective observation. It is necessary to see oneself with other than one's habitual eyes—that is, apart from our usual way of looking at things. Unless we can see ourselves with some impartiality, our fixation on this ego will only continue to block any objective understanding. All that we now call mind and feeling must be observed through new eyes other than our own preferential, egoistic eyes. This new quality of seeing is by means of the eyes of the heart, and the light by which they see is both concentrated and transmitted by an authentic teaching and the resonance of a group.

We have a power of reason that can discern our egoism from our true essential self, and because of this, we have the possibility of transcending our egoism in the name of love and attaining the true meaning of our individuality. A certain energy needs to be produced; a light needs to be kindled within us. Spirit will put a light before us, but we may not recognize it until have taken a step, if only one step, from our egoism.

By keeping the mirror of awareness clear we can begin to free ourselves of our compulsions and inappropriate thoughts and behavior. Presence, conscious awareness is the means; the present moment is the focus. We have certain obstacles to face. We must confront our lack of attention and weakness of will, our attachment to our opinions, our slavery to our likes and dislikes, our perpetual fear of loss. All of these characteristics form the gross material for the work of transformation, to be transformed by the resonance of love, the touchstone of our essential self. It is necessary to awaken and reconnect to this essential self which has the power of love that can tame the false self.

Freedom: Its essential characteristic is having will; a corollary of this is being free of negativity, which frees us from being enslaved to resentment, fear, and other motivators that typically enslave human life. Freedom is being able to do what one chooses without hurting anyone.

Hidden Treasure: The divine qualities latent within the essence of the human being. This is an allusion to the *ḥadīth qudsī* in which God declares, "I was a Hidden Treasure, and I loved to be known." The true human being fulfills a special role in this universe in that he or she has a unique capacity to reflect the Divine Attributes and thus fulfil the ***Amānah*** uniquely entrusted to mankind.

Humbleness: The awareness of our dependence on God, our interdependence, and our need for other human beings. We are not the originators of anything but the reflectors of the attributes of Spirit. All of our qualities, virtues, and capacities have their ultimate source in God, upon whom we depend.

Imaginal: Visionary. The imaginal function is a faculty of the soul that perceives meaning in the form of images. Imaginal must be distinguished from imaginary, which has connotations of illusory. The location of imaginal vision is the *ᶜālam al-mithāl*, the world of the Image, *mundus imaginalis*, while Suhrawardi coined the term *Na-koja-Abad,* the "Land of Nowhere," which corresponds to Thomas More who first used the word "utopia," which means simply "no-place." The plane or level of reality on which imaginal vision functions is a world as ontologically real as the world of the senses and the world of the intellect.

Imagination: (whether referred to as *active*, or *creative*, or *theophanic*): The word *imagination* does not necessarily refer to fantasy or make-believe. Instead imagination is the faculty which perceives spiritual visions. The object of such vision is regarded as real, yet immaterial.

Dr. Jeremy Henzell-Thomas writes: Imagination, and words of this kind, are two-faced, having an authentic and a bogus application, or different levels of description. For example, we could identify three levels of Imagination: firstly, Creative Imagination—a deep "seeing" or "unveiling" (*kashf*) of the archetypal level behind "signs"; secondly, imagination in the artistic sense (the normal positive connotation in our culture); and thirdly, imagination as delusion and destructive fantasy (the "imaginary"), including "whisperings" (as in the Arabic words *ṭāʾif* and *al-wahm*). This last sense also has the sense of suggestibility and susceptibility.

Intellect, ᶜAql: عقل We can distinguish two meanings for "intellect." The first is the partial intellect, or simply thought, mind activated by will and reason—the faculty of mind most under our immediate control. The second is Universal Intellect, the supreme faculty throughwhich we can know the Truth, in the metaphysical sense. Yet, even the partial intellect shares in the attributes of the Universal Intellect.

This Universal Intellect is seen as the seat for the power of discernment; it gives people the ability to see things as they are, to distinguish such attributes as truth and falsehood, beauty and ugliness. However in most humans the intellect is unable to function properly because it is veiled by the ego. The original error in judgment comes from the distorting factor of personal desire, the result of identifying the human spirit with its cloak of water and clay, i.e., the body. Following this mistaken identification, the intellect is unable to penetrate the outward form of those objects within its perceptual field. It only sees the surface of things, not their true nature. If it could go beyond forms to inward meaning, the intellect would discover God in all things. Or as Rumi puts it, "How many words the world contains! But all have one meaning. When you smash the jugs, the water is one."

In most people, the ego dominates the intellect. While veiled, the partial intellect exists in an adversarial relationship with the soul. However in those individuals who are making spiritual progress, the intellect begins to guide and transform the ego. As an individual's ego "thins out," the intellect becomes better at fulfilling its purpose. When the veil of the ego dissolves, the human spirit emerges sanctified. In Rumi's words:

"The partial intellect is a denier of Love, even if it pretends to know the mysteries. It is clever and knowledgeable, but not naughted—as long as the angel is not naughted, it is a demon."

Interdependence: The recognized need of human beings for each other in order to attain the fullness of life on all levels from material to cosmic. Interdependence is a principle that operates on all levels of existence: the physical, chemical, biological, social, and spiritual.

Knowledge, ᶜIlm: علم Seven levels are recognized: knowing something's name; knowing through the senses; knowing about something; knowing through deeper grasp and understanding; knowing through doing; knowing through the supraconscious faculties; direct knowing by means of Spirit alone. Spiritual Knowledge is also known as ᶜirfān.

Leader: Someone, ideally, who is lifted up by others in order to be of service, to get a particular job done, to whom we give love, respect, and whatever necessary to get the job done. The true leader is the one who is in service, not the one who demands to be served. And yet if we respect a leader, we can help her or him to better serve.

Love, Ḥubb: حب The motivating, transforming, and unifying power of Spirit within creation. How Spirit is experienced.

God says, according to the well known *ḥadīth qudsī*: "I was a Hidden Treasure and I loved to be known, so I created the two worlds." Thus all of creation is God's Self-Manifestation, the milieu in which we all exist, which exerts various forces of attraction among all that it contains. Love is the motivating power within God's creation, leading us eventually back to our Source, Allāh. This love (*ḥubb*) motivates the lover (*muḥibb*) to turn toward the Beloved (*maḥbub*).

It is the soul's nature to be impressionable, to take on the qualities of whatever it identifies with, whatever it desires or loves. If it identifies with its social conditioning, it will take on those qualities. If it is identified with miscellaneous desires, it will reflect the contradictions of those desires. If it identifies primarily with its instinct, it takes on animal qualities. If it identifies with Spirit, it takes on the qualities of Spirit.

Whatever the soul chooses to love, it will resemble. And therefore what we choose to love is important: Love is the force behind every level of existence. There is some good in every attraction, but there is a process of refining attraction, of choosing what to love, so that we are energized by a wider, purer love.

At first love operates as attraction or desire, as *eros* (*ᶜishq al-mājazi*), choosing among the many forms that the material world offers. We strive for satisfaction in the emotional and psychological realms. We are identified with the forms we desire, especially through our likes and dislikes, our attractions and our aversions. This love is characterized by love of the desirable, the lovable, and by possessiveness.

Love at another level is sharing with others, or *philos*. There is a beauty just in being able to share a time and a place with others. Relationship broadens the self, tames the ego. Marriage, family, and community form widening spheres of abundant life. *Philos* is sharing and empathy.

But there is a love greater than attraction or sharing, and it is said to be the love for Spirit, objective love, *agape*. Spirit within us can love Spirit in everything. In this love we are loving what we are. It is that close. The duality between you and "the other" has dissolved and what remains is a field of love.

The highest stage of love, *ᶜishq*, is the intense love for God that burns away all other loves of the lover (*ᶜāshiq*).

Love is seeking to manifest Itself and be known. This cosmic milieu in which we exist offers possibilities of bonding, relationship, communion. Our openness, our relatedness, our engagement is a measure of our love. The more we purify ourselves of our self-centeredness, the more we will feel the benefits of this love.

What we find most beautiful, inspiring, magnetic, will draw us out. The experience of love will activate our conscious and subconscious faculties. As our human nervous system develops, it will become a better instrument for sensing beauty.

It is the degree of Spirit in anything that is its beauty. Sometimes we mistake glamor, the imitation of beauty, for real beauty. What is beauty, if it is not purity, radiance, depth?

Spirit is the Life which is behind everything. If we can love that

Spirit, we will more and more find it in ourselves, in others, and in our surroundings, and we will take on Its vivifying qualities.

Lower Self: The self based on ego (*an-nafs al-ʾammārah bis-sū*). See: **False Self.**

Maturity: Wisdom and skillfulness in every aspect of life, which comes from the development and balance of our human faculties and their loving application, which leads to fulfillment in relationships. Maturity is our ability to reflect the Divine Attributes in everyday life.

Meditation, Murāqabah: مراقبة Cultivating pure awareness; listening within; stilling the superficial layers of thought and emotion in order to become aware of the continual awareness which is the ground or foundation of our being. Meditation is a function of consciousness, not of thinking.

The simplest and easiest form of meditation requires two things: a body that is still and relaxed, and an object to focus attention on. Many traditional postures for meditation exist, but the essence of them all is an erect spine and the palms of the hands resting on the knees, or the palms resting upon each other. A focus of attention that may be useful for beginners is the awareness of breathing combined with a mental focus: *Lā ilāha* on the outbreath and *ill Āllāh* on the inbreath. An alternative is: "I" as a feeling in the heart with each inbreath and "am" as a sensation of the whole physical presence on the outbreath. As attention is held on this process, the breathing becomes more calm and the internal dialog begins to settle down. From this position of quiet alertness it becomes possible to view the content of our stream of consciousness. The awareness which in normal living is focused outward gets accustomed to an inward focus. This focus, however, is less on the content than on the process of the mind's activity. Awareness has begun to separate from its identification with the content of experience, both outward experience and inward experience.

In much of our ordinary life we are busy interpreting experience and constructing meanings. Our perceptions are also biased by expectation, opinion, desire, and many other factors. During meditation we use more energy to sustain the process of seeing and very little for interpretation and constructing meanings. The net effect of this kind of meditation practice is that we reduce our reactivity and increase our ability to sustain pure awareness.

At a higher stage of meditation, the focus of awareness becomes more subtle. Instead of focusing on a breath, a sound, or an idea, consciousness attends to *Being* itself. Instead of change, consciousness focuses on that which is changeless, the underlying "Isness." This substratum of consciousness becomes more and more familiar. Instead of the contents of the mirror we are aware of the mirror itself.

Everyday life is seen more and more as a reflection on the mirror—as both real and unreal against the backdrop of this underlying changeless reality. Meditation at this level is experienced as much by a "letting go" as by a firm concentration. As the object of consciousness becomes more subtle, so does the effort of consciousness.

Consciousness attends to whatever arises. Meditation is more and more carried into the gross psychological events of ordinary life. At this stage, some of our compulsions have been recognized and can fall away. The compulsive habits of thought—many of them based on fear, desire, neediness, and self-centeredness—begin to lose their power. The identity which was rooted in these compulsions begins to melt and a new quality of "I" emerges, one based in simple non-reactive awareness. A different less egotistical self begins to be felt.

Freed of our habitual thoughts, expectations, opinions, constructions, and fears, consciousness is free to receive deeper impressions. New meanings begin to flow into consciousness from the unconscious. Extrasensory experience may be heightened. Whether we are aware of it or not, we become more sensitive to other's thoughts and emotions. We may be able to respond to others more sensitively, more wisely, because we are less dominated by our old habitual patterns of thought and feeling. At this stage we are flooded with rich meanings, and life can take on a new depth.

There really is no end to the refinement that is possible. One more and more begins to perceive qualitatively. The ultimate reality, which we are preparing to apprehend and which is all that is, has certain qualities like peace, compassion, creativity, vitality, generosity, glory, subtlety, wisdom, beauty, and unity.

Through this deeper refinement of attention and an evermore subtle focusing, the false self collapses. The support structures it once depended on are gradually removed, and the essential self begins to emerge naturally in full awareness of the Divine Presence.

The spiritual journey or process involves the focusing of attention on ever-subtler levels of Being. It is not, however, the ultimate activity, nor the only tool for spiritual development, but it deserves to be acknowledged as a principle of spiritual living.

Metaphysics: The study of the real nature of things. Metaphysics concerns itself with the nature of body and mind, consciousness, the soul, levels of reality, eternal life, and the ultimate meaning of things.

While informed by the revelation of the Qurʾān which addresses these issues, Islamic metaphysics has also developed a terminology and systematic understanding baased on the "Five Presences": *Hāhūt,* the Divinity in Itself; *Lāhūt,* the Divine when experienced by human beings a the personal God; *Jabarūt,* the realm of angelic powers; *Malakūt,* the world of subtle energies; *Nāsūt,* the human realm.

Both the Qurʾān and the *ḥadīth* testify to the fact that it is within a human being's capacity to know different levels of spiritual reality and that, in fact, this is the inevitable outcome of faith, *īmān.* The principle organ of perception for these spiritual realities is the heart, *al-qalb.*

Mind: Mind is essentially a non-physical phenomenon that has subconscious, conscious, and supraconscious dimensions. The mind is more than its contents, i.e., more than its thoughts and the feelings it registers. It includes our capacities of awareness, attention, intentionality, and will. Although mind is conventionally taken to be our inner psychological life, understanding the true nature of mind will lead us toward an understanding of consciousness itself, and ultimately the Divine.

Mysticism, Taṣawwuf: A capacity peculiar to the human being, which is neither obvious to the intellect nor to the senses, but which depends on the refinement and receptivity of faculties within the supraconscious mind. In English, the word "mysticism" suggests the exploration of the fundamental divine mystery, beyond the reaches of the senses. In Islām *taṣawwuf* signifies purification, especially purification of the heart, by which this "mystery" can to some extent be known.

Pharaoh: A symbol of the ego. Pharaoh claimed to be a god and expected everyone to worship him. According to the Qur᾿ān, Pharaoh asserted, I am your Lord the Most High (Sūrah an-Nāziʿāt 79:24). Moses was given the task freeing God's people from the dominion of Pharaoh. Meanwhile Pharaoh did everything he could to preserve his dominion over them.

From a metaphorical point of view, *Moses* represents the Intellect, *Pharaoh* represents the ego, and *God's people* represents the spirit residing in each person.

Personality: Learned habits of thought, feeling, and behavior; the social self, resembling a mask we wear. In the case of unconscious and spiritually-undeveloped people, personality is often mistaken for one's identity itself. Personality can both manifest the soul or obscure it. In more developed human beings, personality is consciously cultivated to reflect more and more of God's qualities.

Presence: The state of being consciously aware, and thus in alignment with our deepest and highest capacities.

Presence signifies the quality of *consciously being here.* It is the activation of a higher level of awareness which allows all our other human functions—like thought, feeling, and action—to be known, developed, and harmonized. Presence is the way in which we occupy space, as well as how we flow and move. Presence shapes our self-image and emotional tone. Presence determines the degree of our alertness, openness, and warmth. Presence decides whether we leak and scatter our energy or embody and direct it.

Presence is the human self-awareness that is the end result of the evolution of life on this planet. Human presence is not merely quantitatively different from other forms of life; humanity represents a new form of life, of concentrated spiritual energy.

The presence experienced by the human being is actually the presence of Allāh reflected through the human being. We can learn to activate this presence at will. Once activated, we find this presence within and without. Because we find it extending beyond the boundaries of what we thought was ourselves, we are freed from the sense of separation. We could then speak of being *within* this presence.

Prayer: Communication or communion with God. It is conventionally confused with asking something of God, but this is only a limited form of prayer. We have a right to ask God through prayer for our real human and spiritual needs, and there are many forms of prayer increasing in subtlety and intimacy as we open the heart to divine communication.

Prophet, Nabī, Rasūl: نبي، رسول One who brings a Code of Living, a Sacred Law. A prophet may also initiate an elite into knowledge of the Truth.

A *Rasūl* brings a new revelation and religious law. A *Nabī* carries the message within an already existing sacred tradition.

Reality: What we experience as real. There are many realities, or many levels of experience and consciousness possible for the human being, but only one Truth. (See **Truth, *al-Ḥaqq*.**)

Religion: see ***Dīn***. دين

Remembrance: Being aware of the Divine Presence. When the state of presence, or self-awareness, is established in a human being, it then becomes possible to enter into relationship with the Divine Being. See ***Dhikr***.

Revelation, Waḥy, Tanzil: وحي، تنزيل A communication of the Divine Being for the sake of guidance; instructions for the realization of our true human nature from the Source of our human nature; the Holy Books (explicitly: Torah, Psalms, Gospel, Qur'ān; implicitly the sacred books of all traditions).

Self: The self is the sense of identity. At the lowest level it can be a complex of psychological manifestations arising from the body and related to its pleasure and survival. At its highest level it can be experienced as something infinitely subtle and refined. (See also: **Soul; Spirit.**)

Nafs ("soul," "self") is used both for the lower self, and for the immortal soul of a human, which survives death. The self or soul is given by Allāh in a latent or undeveloped form. The purpose of human life is to manifest and develop this "soul" and increase its capacity for relationship with God, even to such an extent that after death it is capable of entering into a higher phase of life and continuing its development.

Service, Khidmah: خدمة The functional outcome of being connected to spiritual energy. It is generally thought to be work performed for others, although a much older meaning was: attention, respect, and devotion.

When we can be aware of the abundance of life, synchronous events unfold in the continuum of time; love brings together what needs to be brought together. Sometimes we find ourselves more clearly in the circumstances of imminent meaning and grace.

The soul's refinement toward a deeper and more continuous presence results in our being able to meet more and more manifestations of Life with unconditional Love. We are able to overcome our separation to such an extent that we feel at one with more and more. Our awareness of our connection with Life increases our sensitivity to our environment and awakens us to more and more opportunities for service, interaction, helpfulness. and we find that our needs are met as well, and the circle continues. In every moment our environment presents us with needs. Our service is the natural outcome—one could almost say the natural consequence—of our awareness of our environment as a whole and our connection with Allāh.

If we find that we are incapable of meeting life with unconditional love, we can at least begin to practice shifting awareness from the preoccupation with ourselves to a wider field of awareness, including the needs of those around us. As we become accustomed to this "shift," opportunities for service arise often and naturally. But service without presence can be marked by a kind of heedlessness, and if we are identified with service, if we expect thanks or some reward, it becomes a subtle demand rather than service.

It is good to do what is right and feel good about it. It is good to serve those whom we love. It is necessary to contribute to the general welfare through generous and public-spirited action. All of this is basic to a decent human life, but it is not yet at the level of spiritual practice.

The service which is spiritual practice is beyond the limited ego. This service depends on a shift of awareness. Through this service we are lifted out of our egoism. In this service we become motivated by unconditional love of life around us. It is Allāh's love loving through us. It is the Generous giving through us.

In contrast to this, even the "service" of those who serve with arrogance or self-righteousness feels like a poison to us. We do not want it, even if we need it.

Service is the outcome of our awareness of the environment as a whole. When we shift from our personal preoccupations to a wider awareness, and if we have overcome the inner pressures of attraction and preference, then we can be more awake to opportunities for service. We can begin to be in the right place at the right time to fill a need.

Any action without presence is unconscious, heedless. The more we undertake in the outer world, the more we need to balance it with a strength of the soul. If we are to truly grow in service we must simultaneously grow in awareness, intention, and love. The more our inner faculties are engaged, the more service will come naturally.

Sigh of Compassion, Nafas ar-Raḥmān: نفس الرحمن Before the creation of the universe, the Divine Names yearned to be known. In His compassion and sympathy for these Names, God is said to have come into existence with a sigh. In other words, it was this sigh of compassion that caused the Names to be epiphanized or manifested in the created universe. Furthermore this sigh continues to preserve the universe by recreating it at each moment.

Sign: see: ***Āyah*** آية

Sin: Sin is essentially a violation against our own or another's humanness. Sin causes separation from God and a veiling of the essential self so that we can no longer perceive the Truth. Sin is saying "no" to God, the opposite of submission. See: **Ẓulm.**

Sincerity, Ikhlāṣ: إخلاص Devotion without self-deception or hypocrisy.

Soul: Individualized Spirit; the non-material essence of the human being; the inner being, which is considered to be eternal. The word "soul" has many different meanings in common English usage, being used almost interchangeably with spirit, mind, conscience, and even heart.

In Islamic spirituality, it is a translation of the word "*nafs*," which also means "self." The soul is the core of individuality which is sustained by Spirit (*Rūḥ*) and in turns sustains the bodily, mental, and emotional functions of the human being. Soul can be strengthened, developed refined, and spiritualized. When the personal self is infused with Spirit, rather than dominated by egoism, we can truly refer to it as the soul.

Spirit, Rūḥ: روح The Life principle which animates all life and especially the human being. On the one hand it is the primary expression of the Divine as it unfolds from Its state of autonomy and creates all of existence. At the same time, it is the transcendent pole of every human being. In other words, while we are individuated here as human beings at the same time we are receiving the animating, spiritualizing force of Spirit. As the Qur'an says: "We breathed into him of Our Spirit." (*Sūrah as-Sajdah* 32:9)

Within our inner life, Spirit is experienced as a transcendent witness. It is that which causes us to speak, to act, to see, when any of these acts are conscious and intentional. Thus anything that we do with presence is an act of the spirit, unlike many of our actions which are motivated by the lower self, and which are typically just automatic, habitual, or reactive. (See also: **Self; Soul.**)

State, Hal: حال A spiritual state or realization which is fleeting or temporary, in contrast to a "station" or *maqām*, which refers to a more stable and enduring spiritual attainment. A state refers to a glimpse of spiritual truths which are more profound than those that characterize a given individual's normal level of realization.

Station, Maqām: مقام Spiritual realization which is relatively stabilized or permanent. One who attains a particular station is said to be established in the truths revealed by that particular level of realization.

Submission, Islām: إسلام Our right relationship with God. The essence of true religion.

At the practical psychological level it is the self (*nafs*) bowing to the Spirit (*Rūḥ*). Listening to the directive of Sprit through the heart. *The true religion with God is islām* (*submission*) (*Sūrah Āl ᶜImrān* 3:19). This verse was revealed before the religion of Islam, as we have come to know it, was established. In the Qur'an, all prophets, including Noah, Moses, Jesus, are referred to as "muslims," those surrendered to God.

Supplication, Duᶜā: دعاء The spontaneous dialog between the worshipper and the Worshipped. See: ***Duᶜā.***

Supraconscious: Faculties of the human mind that are subtle and non-intellectual, a synonym for which is "heart."

Thought, Fikr: فكر A faculty of the mind which forms ideas and synthesizes principles from concrete experience. Thought, however, can be inspired from the higher level of Spirit, or it can be used to justify selfish desires. Thought, therefore, is potentially two-faced, leading the human being either in the direction of Truth or delusion. From Titus Burckhardt: "The faculty which is specific to man is thought (*al-fikr*). Now the nature of thought, like the nature of man, is two-faced. By its power of synthesis it manifests the central position of man in the world and so also his direct analogy with the Spirit. But its formal structure, on the other hand, is only one existential 'style' among many others; that is to say it is a specific mode of consciousness which could be called 'animal' were it not distinguished, for better and for worse, by its connection with man's unique—and intrinsically 'supernatural'—function from those faculties of knowledge that are proper to animal species. In fact thought never plays an entirely 'natural' part in the sense of being a passive equilibrium in harmony with the cosmic surroundings. To the degree that it turns away from the Intellect, which transcends the terrestrial plane, it can only have a destructive character, like that of corrosive acid, which destroys the organic unity of beings and of things."[32]

Truth, Al-Ḥaqq: الحق The Real. For the human being: the knowledge that God is the Truth and that we are intimately related to Him.

Ghazi bin Muḥammad writes in *Truth and Knowledge* (Section 3)a) Truth, (contained in this book): Truth is absolute by nature. This means that something which is true is so completely and utterly, and that its reality exists independently of all knowledge or perception except God's. In other words, something which is true is so, no matter what anybody or everybody says or thinks about it, and conversely, merely thinking about it cannot affect it in any way. This is because truth comes from God's own nature:

That is because God is the Truth! Lo! He quickeneth the dead, and lo! He is Able to do all things (*Sūrah al-Ḥajj* 22:6).

Herein lies the reason why lying is such an offense to God: it is an affront to His Nature which is the Truth. Thus God also says:

Confound not truth with falsehood, nor knowingly conceal the truth. (*Sūrah al-Baqarah*, 2:42)

Universal Intellect, ᶜAql-i Kull: العقل الكلي The intellect that is entirely pure and free of ego, the "Intellect of the intellect." It can discern the meaning hidden within every form, and thus it sees things as they truly are. Although there is only one Universal Intellect, this intellect reveals itself to the saints in varying degrees, according to their capacity.

The Unseen, Ghayb: غيب Those aspects of reality we have veiled ourselves from; the reality behind appearances, comprised of qualities, intelligence, and will.

Will, Irādah: إرادة The ability to act consciously; the faculty of conscious choice; a power of the soul by which we can direct our thoughts, actions, and, eventually, even our feelings. Will is directly connected with Spirit. It is a unique attribute of the human being, because no other creature, as far as we know, has this degree of conscious choice. Will

---

[32] Titus Burckhardt, *An Introduction to Sufism*, chapter 15, *The Intellectual Faculties*.

enables us to rise above personal desire and egoistic satisfactions.

Human will is derived from the divine will as the image in a mirror is a reflection of the source of that image. Human will is a dim reflection of the divine will. The human being, then, is the mirror of God's will. As we develop spiritually we begin to see how our own will is related to Will of the Divine.

In traditional spiritual education, a disciple (*murīd*) is someone who is *willing* to accept the demands of the discipline they have committed themselves to. The willing *murīd* steps beyond his or her own individual limitations. In a sense, the *murīd* must give up his own habitual will, which was based on the desires of the ego, in order to develop a new level of will. A *murīd* derives this will from the spiritual dimension by consciously choosing to submit to that higher spiritual power. The sincere spiritual seekers are *those who call upon their Lord morning and evening seeking (willing, yurīdūna) His Face* (*Sūrah al-Anᶜām* 6:52).

An even higher level is the *murad*, the one *who is willed*, i.e., someone through whom the divine attributes can express themselves, someone overflowing with *baraka*, the divine grace.

Will develops as we make conscious choices and bring those conscious choices and decisions to completion. In other words, our fulfilling of our responsibilities develops our will; whereas every uncompleted decision drains us of will. Will is a capacity that we must continually preserve and maintain, if we are to be fully human.

"Great numbers who quarrel with their condition have lacked not the Power but the Will to obtain a better State" (Samuel Johnson).

Wisdom, Ḥikmah: حكمة Knowledge which comes from within. Wisdom is related to justice, which is putting everything in its proper place. Wisdom is a quality gained from experience that enables action appropriate to the situation. See: **Ḥikmah.**

Witnessing, Mushāhadah: مشاهدة The direct perception, vision, or knowing of Reality. The witnessing of Allāh in all things. It is the capacity at the heart of meditation. The *Shahādah*, or testimony of faith, implies that we have a direct perception, and not just a nominal assent, to what is witnessed.

Yearning, Shawq: شوق the intense longing to be near the Beloved, Allāh. Yearning is one of the most valuable attributes of a human being, which becomes the motivating force of the whole journey of return to God. Yearning is an expression of hope. *For those who hope to meet Allāh, the term appointed by Allāh is surely coming* (*Sūrah al-ᶜAnkabūt* 29:5).

Appendices

Appendix A

The Arabic Root QWM

Some convergences with English words

Jeremy Henzell-Thomas

The range of meanings associated with the root QWM in the Qur' ān are (according to the Kasssis Concordance):

qāma	vb.	to keep vigil, to arise, to rise; to halt, to stand up, to stand over; to come to pass; (with prep. *li-*) to secure something for someone; (with prep. *bi-*) to uphold. (n.vb.) the act of standing, rising. (pcple. act.) one who is standing; coming to pass; (with prep. *bi-)* one who is upholding, one who performs (a duty)
maqām	n.m.	a place, station; the act of standing
muqām	n.m.	an abode
qawām	n.m.	a just stand
qawīm	n.m.	(adj. comp. *aqwam;* pl. *qiyām)* standing, upright, erect, straight
qawm	n.m.	people, folk
qawwām	n.m.	a manager; (with prep. *bi-)* a securer, one who is staunch
qayyim	n.m.	(*qiyam*, in 6:161; f. *qayyimah*, in 98:5) right, true
qayyūm	n.m.	(adj) Everlasting, Eternal
qiyām	n.m.	the act of maintaining or managing; an establishment, a standard; an asylum
qiyāmah	n.f.	resurrection (*yawm al-qiyāmah*)
qawwama	vb.	(n.vb.) symmetry, stature
aqāma	vb.	to abide; to set or set up; to perform (*aqāma as-ṣalāt*, "to perform the prayer"); to maintain; to assign; (*aqāma al-wazn*, in 55:9, "to set up the balance," hence "to weigh with justice"). (n.vb.) the act of performing (the prayer); the act of abiding. (pcple.act.) one who performs (the prayer); that which remains, lasting
istaqāma	vb.	to go straight; (pcple. act.) straight

There is a clear association here between the notion of *firm establishment/permanence* (abiding, abode, uphold, keep vigil, staunch, maintain, secure, perform—as in the sense of establishing the prayer, resurrection) with the notion of *straightness* "straight, erect, upright, standing" and *truth* "right, true."

Aristotle makes the connection between goodness, happiness, and the perfect cube (firmly established, stable, secure, straight-edged): "The good man [and hence in Aristotle's ethics a "happy" man, because true happiness is contingent on goodness] is a perfect cube."

The etymology of the English word *right* takes us back to the hypothetical Indo-European base reg- "move in a straight line," hence "direct." The base also produced English *rich* and Latin *rex* "king" (source of English *royal* and *regal*). Combination with the past participial suffix *-to-* resulted in Latin *rectus* "straight, right" which lies behind English *rectify, rectitude, rectangle, rector,* and prehistoric German *rekhtaz* which has evolved into German and Dutch *recht*, Swedish *ratt*, Danish *ret*, and English *right*. The use of the word as the opposite of *left* in English, German, and Dutch (but not in the Scandinavian languages) derives from the notion that the right hand is the "correct" hand to use. The derived *righteous* etymologically means "in the right way"; it was compounded in the Old English period from *riht* "right" and *wis* "way." We also have *regular, regulation, regiment,* etc., from the same root.

The following constellation of meanings can be associated with the the word "right": *right* (in two senses—*correct* and the *opposite of left*), *royal, regal, righteous, upright* (note the two senses in English—"standing up straight," "erect," and "honourable") *direct, rectify, rectitude* ("moral uprightness," "righteousness"), *"right-angled."* The sense "opposite of left" is particularly interesting in the context of the notion of the "two hands of God" and the metaphysical schemes drawn up around the dichotomy left/right by Ibn al-ᶜArabī and others. *Straight,* itself a fascinating word which has various connotations—"without curve or bend," "going direct to the mark" (in New Testament Greek, "sin" (*hamartia*) is "missing the mark," and in *Sūrah Āl ᶜImrān* 3:8 there is the prayer: *Let not our hearts swerve/deviate from the Truth*); "upright, honest, candid, not evasive" (as in "straight-talking," "straight-dealing," or "straightforward"); "logical, not swayed by emotion" (thinking "straight"); "in proper order, place, or condition, duly arranged, level, symmetrical" (is my hair "straight"? to "straighten out a problem"). Note also the connection in English between "crooked" and "dishonest" (in English slang a "bent copper" is a corrupt policeman, and to "go straight" is to abandon crime after a stretch in prison).

Interestingly the word "steadfastness," another word used to translate *istaqama,* is derived from the prehistoric Germanic *stadiz* (modern German *stadt,* "town") which goes back to Indo-European *stetis,* a derivative of the base *ste-, sta-,* "stand" which also produced Latin *stare,* "stand" (source of English *state* and *station*). The *-fast* part of the word *steadfast* comes from Germanic *fastuz,* "firm." So once again, this English word covers the meanings "stand firmly, abide in a state or station" which reflects perfectly many of the Arabic meanings of the QWM root. Note the sense of "stand" as in "standing up for someone or for what we believe"—a sense of moral courage.

Given all this, it can be understood why the concept of *istaqama* is often referred to as the key to Islām. What is especially interesting is how the English language, with its multiple connotations around the related notions of "straight" and "right," is able to do just what Arabic does, although the implicit meanings can often only be recovered through etymological investigation. Furthermore, the English connotations open up the association of "right" with the "right hand" and the left/right dichotomy/complementarity.

It is also striking how the Classical (Greek and Latin) roots in English are pregnant with universal meanings which often capture the same constellation of meanings as Arabic words dealing with the same concepts. I have a sense here of a *universal* language of related concepts, e.g., in English and Arabic the sense "upright" has the connotation of the *standing physical posture* and *righteousness.* There is something *objective* here, something about the very structure of the human being, and the relationship between his body, soul, and spirit.

For me there is another angle, a more mysterious one, something ineffable. That is the mystery of the curved, the feminine, the left hand. If the path we are enjoined to follow is the "straight" path, and this is associated with right (in both senses of correctness and the right hand), truth, righteousness, clear (as opposed to allegorical) messages, firm establishment, steadfastness, then there is a danger, if we must use Jungian terms, that we fail to do the work on the "shadow" and the "anima," or in Hillman's language, that we become too "vertical," too "transcendent," too taken up into the masculine clarity of Apollo or the realm of Zeus, the sky god, ultimately "wrathful," "*self*-righteous," "overbearing" (rather than the more positive "standing over" implied by the QWM root). We will lose our connection with the wet places of the earth, the horizontal dimension of the feminine.

Interestingly, this imbalance is reflected in the negative connotations of words derived from the archaic English word "strait," meaning "narrow, limited, confining"—e.g., *strait-laced* (severely virtuous or scrupulous, puritanical); *strait-jacket.* The word *strait* derives from *strict* which was acquired direct from *strictus,* the past participle of Latin *stringere, "pull tight"* (source of English *stringent* and *strain*). Routed via Old French, *strictus* has also given English *stress* and *stricture,* as well as prefixed forms *constrain, constrict, distress, restrain, and restrict.* Note also the negative connotations of words connected with the idea of "right"and derived from the reg- base, e.g., *regulations* (with their sense of the *unbending*), and *regiment* (as a verb, to "regiment" someone).

What is revealing here is that the English word *straight* began life as the past participle of *stretch.* In Middle English this was *straught,* whence the adjective *straight.* The sense of "not bent or curved" derives from the notion of stretching something between two points. So there is a semantic connection between *straight* and *strict,* both being derived from the underlying idea of "stretching tight."

The subtle negative connotations contained within their variant forms give us warnings about the need for balance. So the "straight" path must not become the "strict" path, that which "straitens" and "constricts" us. There must be both expansion and contraction (*basṭ/qabḍ).* Too much "straitening" is the over-masculinisation of the way, a turning too far to the right (note the political connotation of the "right," implying authoritarian conservatism and severity).

Appendix B

A Pedagogy for Exploring a Divine Name

Jeremy Henzell-Thomas

Al-Quddūs

The essential concept in the Arabic root *QDS* is to be "far removed." Thus,

qadusa	to be holy, pure; to hallow, sanctify, dedicate, consecrate, declare to be holy, hold sacred, venerate, revere.
quds, qudus	holiness, sacredness, sanctity, sanctuary, shrine (*al-Quds* = Jerusalem)
qudsī	holy, sacred, hallowed
qudsīya, qadāsa	holiness, sacredness, sanctity
taqdīs	sanctification, consecration, reverence, veneration
muqaddis	reverent, reverential
muqaddas, mutaqaddis	hallowed, sanctified, sacrosanct, holy, sacred

It is valuable to explore the English words here. *Holy* and *hallowed* come from a prehistoric Germanic adjective which gives us English *whole,* and so its etymological meaning is "unimpaired, inviolate." This has exactly the sense of "freedom from any defect" associated with *al-Quddūs,* or, as Al-Ghazālī says, "free of what sense can perceive or imagination conceive" and, furthermore, transcending any concept of perfection we might have. The sense *"whole"* behind the English word *holy* points to the fact that only that which is whole is truly holy, and only God is Whole.

The word *sacred* comes from Latin *sacer,* which comes from a base which produced Latin *sancire* "consecrate," source of English *saint, sanctuary, sanctity,* etc. Related to the same base are "sacrament," "sacrosanct," and "sacrifice" (from a Latin compound meaning to "make holy").

The word *revere* goes back ultimately to Latin *vereri*, "hold in awe or fear," which, interestingly, may be a distant relative of English *aware* and *beware*, thus etymologically connecting holy awe with consciousness and "guarding" (exactly the sense of *taqwā*). *Al-Quddūs* is traditionally associated with the Names of Majesty (*jalāl*), rather than Beauty, i.e., those Names which express the incomparability (*tanzīh*), inaccessibility (*ʿizza*) and distance (*buʿd*) of God (*utterly remote in His limitless glory*), rather than His "similarity" (*tashbīh*) and nearness (*closer to you than your jugular vein*), and the human response to the Names of Majesty is that of awe (*hayba*) and fear (*khawf*).

This uncovering of related meanings through etymology is tremendously valuable as a means of opening up the underlying concepts contained in the root and its English equivalents. By doing this we can also tease out fresh educational implications, and it is wholly in keeping with our aim of expressing universal Qurʾānic concepts in English.

Educational implications

It seems to me that our essential task in reflecting on the Names is to generate some fresh insights which can be *of use* to students in understanding the Names *in relation to their own lives.* "I seek refuge in God from a knowledge which has no use," said the Prophet ﷺ. The linguistic/etymological approach is capable of uncovering a lot of fresh material which is directly applicable to our educational objectives, and it will be productive to develop this methodology in relation to the other Names.

The following teaching points can be deduced from the linguistic analysis of *Al-Quddūs* and English equivalents:

1. *Al-Quddūs* is beyond anything that our senses can perceive or our imagination can conceive, and transcends any concept of perfection which we might have. So we can only approach *Al-Quddūs* by freeing ourselves, as Al-Ghazālī says, from "all fanciful, tangible, and imagined things" and refreshing ourselves with universal, divine knowledge which is concerned with "eternal and everlasting objects of knowledge, *not with changeable and imaginable individuals.*"

Teaching points

The concept of an unreachable perfection applies *only to God*, and not to the activities or ambitions of man. Failure to understand this has led to many modern ills, e.g., the quest for the "perfect" body (and attendant illnesses like anorexia), the "perfect" relationship, and now increasingly the "perfect" home or "perfect" garden. Examples of all these illusory "perfections" can be found all around us.

Guide students towards an understanding of the transitoriness and imperfection of "changeable and imaginable individuals" (e.g., "celebrities" and media "icons"). Help them also to realize that an over-valuation of the artistic achievements of man is actually preventing them from developing even higher faculties of perception which can approach nearer to *Al-Quddūs* even though they can never fully grasp His perfection. But this is an advanced lesson—let them *first* develop creative imagination and aesthetic refinement through literature and the arts, while developing discernment about the moral and spiritual purpose of true, objective art as opposed to "art" reduced to the level of "personal expression," ephemeral fashion, or egotistical self-indulgence.

2. *Al-Quddūs* evokes the human response of holy awe, veneration and reverence towards that which is beyond our comprehension.

Teaching points

Develop a sense of reverence and wonder in students. This can be done through all subjects, e.g., through science (not only through understanding the order and harmony of scientific laws but also in understanding the *limitations* of science in being unable to tell us about that part of reality which is unobservable (the "Unseen"), and through being with and contemplating Nature. We live in increasingly cynical times—that open-eyed sense of wonder in small children (which is part of *fiṭrah*) is quickly extinguished. We must, as a sacred trust, feed and nourish that sense of wonder and reverence in young minds and hearts. And not only that sense of reverence and wonder in the face of Nature but also in the presence of all other human beings, whose sacredness should always be respected.

3. To enter into the *sacred, sacrosanct* Presence, the *sanctuary* of *Al-Quddūs,* requires a *sacrifice.*

Teaching Points

Help students understand that the way to the Presence of God, like all noble objectives, requires the *leaving behind* of those undesirable traits of character which are incompatible with the objective. This theme can be explored in all kinds of ways with students, drawing on their own personal experience of necessary sacrifices. Explore the idea of the "sacred space," the "sanctuary," and what must be left behind to enter it. Explore the idea of prayer as a sacred act within a sacred space, with the prerequisite of purification.

4. *Al-Quddūs* is whole ("holy"), a unity.

Teaching points

Explore the connection between "holiness" and "wholeness."

Explore the idea of the holiday (i.e., a "holy day") and its connection with "resting" and "re-creation," as opposed to the violation of this holistic concept in its increasing use for more and more frenetic activity, shopping, work, etc. (more and more shops are open on Sundays and shop-workers are not even getting to be with their own families at weekends).

5. The very remoteness of *Al-Quddūs* is what makes us travel, both outwardly and inwardly, drawing us ever onwards in the hope that we may be admitted into the divine Presence.

Teaching points

Teach students to have the highest expectations of themselves, to believe that anything is possible, that they can travel to the farthest horizons, not in the sense of trying to become "perfect" themselves, but in the sense of believing they are capable, with God's grace, of achieving their spiritual destiny as servants of God. High expectations must be coupled with humility and modesty, so as to counter arrogance.

Many more educational implications and their practical applications in the classroom could be drawn out from each Name in this way. The possibilities are vast!

Bibliography

Abdel Haleem, Muhammad. *Understanding the Qur'an: Themes and Style.* London: I.B.Tauris. 1999.

Asad, Muhammad. *The Message of the Qur'an.* Bristol: The Book Foundation. 2005.

Al-Attas, Syed Muhammad Naquib. *Islam and Secularism.* Kuala Lampur: International Institute of Islamic Thought and Civilization. 1993.

Ayoub, Mahmoud M. *The Qur'an and Its Interpreters.* Albany, New York: State University of New York Press. 1992.

Badri, Malik. *Contemplation: An Islamic Psychospiritual Study.* Herndon, Vrginia: The International Institute of Islamic Thought. 2000.

Bennabi, Malik. *The Qur'anic Phenomenon.* Translated by El-Mesawi. Kuala Lampur: Islamic Book Trust. 2001.

Eaton, Charles Le Gai. *Islam and the Destiny of Man.* Albany: State University of New York. 1985.

Gatje, Helmut. *The Qur'an and Its Exegesis.* Oxford, England: One World. 1996.

Glassé, Cyril. *The Concise Encyclopedia of Islam.* San Francisco: Harper San Francisco. 1989.

Izutsu, Toshihiko. *Ethico-Religious Concepts in the Qur'an.* Montreal: McGill University Press. 1966.

Kamali, Mohammad Hashim. *Freedom of Expression in Islam.* Cambridge: Islamic Texts Society. 1994.

Kassis, Hannah E. *A Concordance of the Qur'an.* Berkeley: University of California Press, 1983.

Lane, E.W. *Arabic-English Lexicon.* Cairo: Thesaurus Islamicus Foundation. 2003.

Al Qushayri, *Principles of Sufism.* Translated by B.R. Von Schlegel. Berkeley: Mizan Press. 1990.

Rahman, Fazlur. *Islam.* Chicago: The University of Chicago Press. 1979

Rahman, Fazlur. *Major Themes of the Qur'an.* Chicago: Bibliotheca Islamica. 1980.

Watt, W. Montgomery. *Bell's Introduction to the Qur'an: Completely Revised and Enlarged.* Edinburgh Universit Press. 1970.

At **The Book Foundation** our goal is to express the highest ideals of Islam and the Qur'an through publications, curricula, and other learning resources, suitable for schools, parents, and individuals, whether non-Muslims seeking to understand the Islamic perspective, or Muslims wanting to deepen their understanding of their own faith. Please visit our website: **thebook.org**

The Book of Revelations

A Sourcebook of Themes from the Holy Qur'an,

Edited by Kabir Helminski

$33 £16.95 6 x 9" 508pp

1-904510-12-4

This book invites us to recognize and reflect upon the essential spiritual themes of the Qur'an. It offers 265 titled selections of ayats, presented in a fresh contemporary translation of high literary quality, with accompanying interpretations by Muhammad Asad, Yusuf Ali, and others. It is an essential sourcebook for Muslims and non-Muslims alike.

The Book of Character

An Anthology of Writings on Virtue from Islamic and Other Sources

Edited by Camille Helminski

$33 £16.95 6 x 9" 484pp

1-904510-09-4

A collection of writings dealing with the qualities of our essential Human Nature: Faith and Trust; Repentance and Forgiveness; Compassion and Mercy; Patience and Forbearance; Modesty, Humility, and Discretion; Purity; Intention and Discernment; Generosity and Gratitude; Courage, Justice, and Right Action; Contentment and Inner Peace; Courtesy and Chivalry. From the Prophets Abraham and Moses, to the sages Confucius and Buddha, to the Prophet Muhammad, his wife, Khadija, and his companions Abu Bakr and 'Ali, through great saints like Rumi, and humanitarians like Florence Nightingale, Mother Theresa, and Martin Luther King, and even in the personal story of the bicyclist Lance Armstrong, we find stories and wisdom that will help us toward spiritual well-being.

The Book Foundation *has embarked on an important effort to develop books and teaching tools that are approachable and relevant to Muslims and non-Muslims.* ~**Shabbir Mansuri**, *Founding Director, Council on Islamic Education (CIE)*

The Book of Essential Islam

The Spiritual Training System of Islam
Ali Rafea,
with Aisha and Aliaa Rafea
$21 £10.95 6 x 9" 276 pp
1-904510-13-2

This book examines the main teachings and practices of Islam with lucidity and depth. It is a corrective to the distortions and misconceptions of Islam that abound. It can serve equally well to introduce non-Muslims to Islam, as well as to enhance Muslims understanding of their own faith. This book presents Islam as a spiritual training system that supports us in harmonizing ourselves with the Divine Order and thus with each other and our environment. It reveals the intent and inner significance of practices like ablution, ritual prayer, fasting, and pilgrimage.

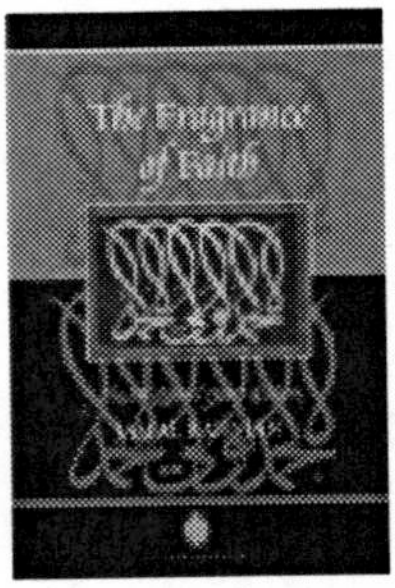

The Fragrance of Faith

The Enlightened Heart of Islam
Jamal Rahman
$15.95 £9.95 6 x 9" 176pp
1-904510-08-6

The Fragrance of Faith reveals the inner Islam that has been passed down through the generations. Jamal is a link in this chain, passing along the message, just as he received it from his grandfather, a village wiseman in Bangladesh. We need reminders of this "enlightened heart of Islam" in our lives, our homes, and our schools. In Jamal Rahman's book Islam is alive and well. ~**Imam Feisal Abdul Rauf**, Author *Islam: A Sacred Law* and *What's Right With Islam*.

This heartfelt book is perfect for the classroom, whether in a Muslim context, or outside of it. It conveys a tradition of compassion and humor passed through one family that represents the best Islam has to offer. And Mr. Rahman is highly entertaining. ~**Michael Wolfe**, *The Hadj: An American's Pilgrimage to Mecca*, Producer of the PBS Documentary: *Muhammad: The Legacy of a Prophet*.

The Book of Nature

A Sourcebook of Spiritual Perspectives on Nature and the Environment

Camille Helminski (Author)

This anthology of spiritual treatments of nature and the environment presents an uplifting and universal approach to appreciating the natural order from a Muslim perspective. Each chapter is introduced with a passage from the Qur'an and followed by pieces that highlight the human role in maintaining balance in the world. Selections range from poems to short essays and cover topics such as unity, interdependence, communication, the four elements, diversity, and wonder. Including contributions from Muhammad Asad, Alain de Botton, Thomas Berry, Guy Eaton, Seyyid Hossein Nasr, and Vandana Shiva, these reminders of the power of the Divine Order allow for a deeper appreciation of the interdependence of life and nature.

Camille Helminski is the author of *Women of Sufism, The Book of Character, The Light of Dawn*, and numerous translations. She is the first woman to translate and publish a significant portion of the Qur'an.

Price: $32.95
Pages: 500
Book Type: Paper
Size: 6 x 9
ISBN: 1904510159

The Message of the Qur'an

by Muhammad Asad

- Newly designed and typeset
- Available in two formats: a single hardback volume, and a boxed set of six parts in paperback for ease of handling and reference
- Original artwork by the internationally renowned Muslim artist and scholar, Dr. Ahmed Moustafa
- A Romanised transliteration of the Arabic text
- A newly compiled general index

As the distinguished British Muslim, Gai Eaton, explains in a new Prologue to the work, there is no more useful guide to the Qur'an in the English language than Muhammad Asad's complete translation and commentary, and no other translator has come so close to conveying the meaning of the Qur'an to those who may not be able to read the Arabic text or the classical commentaries. Generous sponsorship has enabled the Foundation to offer this work at a very reasonable price for a publication of this exceptional quality.

Price: Hardback $55, £28, 39 Euros
Boxed set of 6 deluxe paperback volumes: $60, £33, 45 Euros
ISBN: Hardback 1-904510-00-0 Boxed set 1-904510-01-9
Hardback cover size: 8.5 x 11. Approximately: 1200 pages

To Order In the USA:
The Book Foundation: 831 685 3995
Bookstores: IPG 800 888 4741
In England: Orca Book Services 01202 665432

Or visit our website: TheBook.org